To Mr Tom Hockaday
With best compliments from

Dr. Mohamed Musa Al Yousef

27. 4. 2014

Oil and the
Transformation
of Oman
1970-1995

The Socio-Economic Impact

Oil and the Transformation of Oman 1970-1995

The Socio-Economic Impact

Mohamed bin Musa Al-Yousef

STACEY INTERNATIONAL
LONDON

Oil and the Transformation of Oman
1970-1995
by Mohamed bin Musa Al-Yousef

Published by Stacey International
128 Kensington Church Street, London W8 4BH

British Library Cataloguing-in-Publication Data
A catalogue record for this book is available from the British Library

ISBN 0 905743 857 cased edition
ISBN 0 905743 873 paperback

Set by SX Composing, Rayleigh, Essex

Printing and binding by Oman Printers and Stationers Ltd.

Dedication

This study is dedicated to the enlightened leader and fountainhead of development in Oman, His Majesty Sultan Qaboos bin Said, whose clarity of vision and foresight has inspired the course of development in the Sultanate, and to all those involved – directly or indirectly – in the process of the socio-economic transformation of Oman.

A special word of gratitude and admiration goes to my mother, Mariam bint Moosa Abdul Latiff, whose solid support, encouragement and sacrifices in the early 1960s – when education in Oman was a luxury, food was scarce and living conditions were extremely difficult – laid the foundation in me for a continuous quest for education and enlightenment.

Contents

Chapter Three

The Role of Oil in the Growth and Structural Transformation of the Economy

Chapter Four

Oil and the Human Dimension of Development

Chapter Five

Overall Assessment and Conclusion

Appendices

List of tables

11

List of charts

Chapter Four

List of abbreviations

FYP	Five-Year Development Plan, also referred to as Five-Year Plan
GDP	Gross Domestic Product
GNP	Gross National Product
HM	His Majesty
ILO	International Labour Organisation
OAPEC	Organisation of Arab Petroleum Exporting Countries
OECD	Organisation for Economic Co-operation and Development
OPEC	Organisation of Petroleum Exporting Countries
PDO	Petroleum Development (Oman) Ltd
RO	Rial Omani, also Omani Rial
SGRF	State General Reserve Fund
UNDP	United Nations Development Programme
UNESCO	United Nations Educational, Scientific and Cultural Organization
UNICEF	United Nations Children's Fund
US$	United States of America Dollar

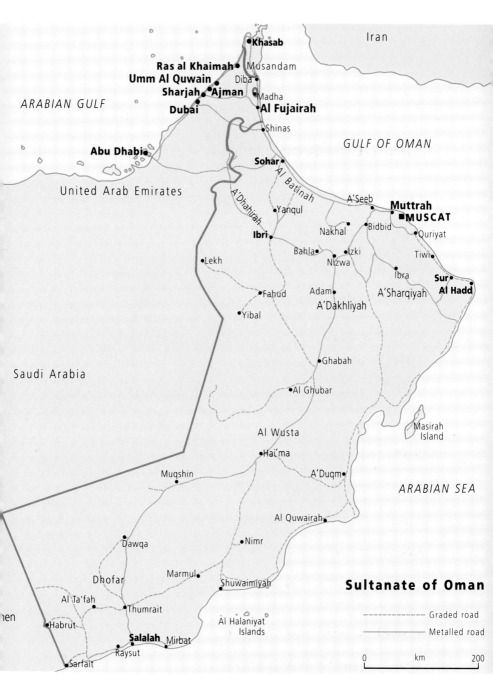

Iran

Khasab

Ras al Khaimah • Musandam
Umm Al Quwain Diba
Sharjah • **Ajman** Madha
Dubai **Al Fujairah**

ARABIAN GULF

• Shinas

GULF OF OMAN

Abu Dhabi

Sohar •
Al Batinah

United Arab Emirates

A'Seeb
A'Dhahirah • Yanqul **Muttrah**
■MUSCAT
Nakhal Bidbid
Ibri • Quriyat
Bahla • Izki Tiwi
• Lekh Nizwa
Ibra **Sur**
Al Hadd
Adam A'Sharqiyah
• Fahud
A'Dakhliyah
• Yibal

Saudi Arabia

• Ghabah

• Al Ghubar

Masirah
Island
Al Wusta

• Hai'ma

Muqshin A'Duqm
ARABIAN SEA

Al Quwairah

Dawqa • Nimr

Dhofar Marmul •
Shuwaimiyah

Al Ta'fah Al Halaniyat
nen Thumrait Islands
•Habrut

Salalah Mirbat
Sarfait Raysut

Sultanate of Oman

- - - - Graded road
———— Metalled road

0   km   200

15

Introduction

Until 23rd July, 1970, and the assumption of power by His Majesty Sultan Qaboos bin Said, little was known in most parts of the world, including some Arab countries, about the recent history of the Sultanate of Oman, despite its rich and diversified history dating back to the third millennium BC.

Prior to 1970, Oman was firmly rooted in the past – a result of the deliberate policy of the previous Sultan, Said bin Taimur, and the lack of any real income prior to the export of oil in 1967. However, even when this income began to flow in, it was not reflected in the economic and social development of the country, mainly because of the Sultan's innate caution and partly due to funding the war in Dhofar – a point which we shall elaborate in Chapter One.

In fact, Oman pre-1970 was a classic underdeveloped country, having almost all of the key structural features of underdeveloped economies as articulated by a number of leading development economists such as Prebisch, Hans Singer, Dudley Seers and Myrdal.[1] These are:

a A traditional, largely agricultural sector using technology with low levels of productivity, and a modern sector – oil in the case of Oman – using much more advanced technology.

b A modern sector established by foreign capital engaged in primary production for export.

c A modern sector characterised by a high degree of openness (i.e. all its output is exported and almost all of its requirements – both for capital equipment and manufactured goods – are imported).

d A modern sector employing a very small proportion of the total population.

The rebirth of Oman began in 1970 – the year of Renaissance – when, under the wise and dedicated leadership of His Majesty Qaboos bin Said, fourteenth head of the Al-Said dynasty, the country embarked on immediate implementation of a comprehensive programme of reform in health services, education and economic development – aimed at bringing the country into the twentieth century.

The present day Oman, for those who knew it before 1970, now evokes a sense of wonder and achievement. The vast majority of the Omani population (almost 51 per cent of whom are under twenty)[2] – who have experienced nothing except the rapid pace of development under His Majesty, now take for granted what they consider as the norm.

A common expression heard in Oman is, 'Before Qaboos – nothing', and it is true that for many Omanis the country was reborn on 23rd July, 1970.

Although Oman's development strategy – which was approved by the Development Council in 1975 – emphasised the important role of the market in the development process, the initial condition of acute underdevelopment prevailing then – to which we have referred earlier – prevented Oman from adopting the doctrine of *laissez-faire* advocated by the neo-classical school.[3] There was no alternative to a substantial degree of state intervention in order to achieve a satisfactory rate of resource mobilisation for economic development. This is in line with almost all early writers on economic development, such as Hirschman, Leibenstein and Myrdal. A notable exception is Peter Bauer, who pointed either explicitly or implicitly, to the failure of the static theory of comparative advantage to provide the correct basis for long-run resource allocation strategies in primary exporting economies.[4]

The purpose of this study, therefore, is to discuss and review how the government, through a 'market-friendly' strategy, developed the oil resources which in turn were judiciously applied, through an effective but limited government activism, to the transformation of a nation from, as it were, nothing to become a respected member of the international community within 20 years; how, as **Appendix Table VII.1** shows, a social infrastructure of health, education, communications and a diversified economic base were created from a non-existent one.

The study will also attempt to illustrate how an underdeveloped economy was able to achieve the dual goals of growth and human development by adopting development planning – at a time when the whole discipline of development economics was under attack, both by leading economists for its failure to address the problems of poverty and inequality, and by the neo-classical counter-revolutionaries who were calling for, *interalia*, the dismantling of planning in developing countries.

It is important to mention, however, that although Oman is an oil producing country, neither its reserves nor its annual production are as high as its neighbours. Relative to the size of the country and its population the oil reserves are indeed very insignificant. As we shall see in Chapter Two, per capita oil production in Oman is less than one-third of that of its immediate neighbour in the Gulf Co-Operation Council – the United Arab Emirates.

Apart from limited resources relative to its neighbours, other problems – such as those associated with the particular stage of Oman's demographic transition, constraints arising out of deteriorating terms of trade, and the relatively long time span required to achieve sustainable development – will also be discussed in this study.

The book's subject matter is divided into five chapters. **Chapter One** provides an overview of the geography and history of Oman, as this is an essential prerequisite for an understanding of the past socio-economic picture of Oman as compared to the neighbouring countries of the Arabian peninsula. This chapter brings out the distinct character of Oman, its ancient heritage and the stagnant socio-economic settings pre-July, 1970, when the present HM Sultan Qaboos came to power. **Chapter Two** discusses the dilemmas faced by a resource-based economy in terms of resource development and allocation, terms of trade and oil price instability and the strategies that were adopted to deal with them. **Chapter Three** focuses on the impact of oil revenues on the development process. It also attempts to trace the linkages between growth of oil revenues and economic change, and the important role of government intervention in achieving the goals of the development strategy. **Chapter Four** provides an overview of the achievements in the field of human resource development in terms of health and education and illustrates how appropriate growth policies can aid human development. **Chapter Five** provides an overall assessment of the development process, and also outlines some of the issues facing Oman as it enters the twenty-first century.

Annexure tables and reference notes are placed at the end of each chapter, while some statistical tables, important documents and a selected bibliography are included as Appendices.

1   Hunt (1989), pp.49-50 and pp.121-22.
2   Oman, *Fourth FYP* (1991), p.142.
3   Hunt (1989), p.44.
4   Ibid., p.52.

Chapter One

Geographical, Social and Historical Background

Oman is a country in which change has collided with permanence at unprecedented speed. Two and a half decades of hard work and dedicated leadership have brought Oman economic and social development, social and racial harmony, progress towards participative government and a positive place in the world. There can be no understanding of what these achievements mean to the Omani people without a brief consideration of the period prior to the watershed year of 1970, the aim of which is to provide a background and perspective to the developments that followed thereafter.

The geographical background is an essential prerequisite to the understanding of Oman, as it illustrates the difference between the Sultanate and the remainder of the Arabian Peninsula in terms of geography and people, and provides an explanation for much of the country's history.

The historical background will, I hope, demonstrate the backwardness of the country at the time of assumption of power by His Majesty in 1970.

1.1 Geographical and social background

The Sultanate of Oman, which covers an area of almost 309,000 sq. kms., occupies most of the south-eastern part of the Arabian peninsula between latitudes 16° 40' and 26° 20'N and longitudes 51° 50' and 59° 40' E. It has a coastline of some 1,700 kms., facing the Gulf of Oman and the Arabian Sea. Its neighbours are the United Arab Emirates (UAE) to the north-west, Saudi Arabia to the west, and the Arab Republic of Yemen to the south-west. The northernmost part of Oman, the Musandam peninsula, is separated from the main part of the country by a strip of land some 80 kms. wide, forming part of the UAE. The Musandam peninsula commands the strategically important Strait of Hormuz through which oil tankers pass carrying most of the oil exported from the Gulf.

The geography of Oman has affected its history and its people. Both have developed separately from the remainder of the peninsula. To quote Pridham:

'Oman has undoubted fascination for observers of the Arab Gulf for two main reasons. One is that it is so obviously different from all its neighbours: general statements about the Arab Gulf, whether in modern times or distant history, usually require qualification as far as Oman is concerned. The list of differences is, if not endless, at least all embracing. Oman above all, is not even in the Arab Gulf. Its enormously long coastline (about 1,700 kms) lies almost entirely on the Gulf of Oman and the Indian Ocean, while a mere 50 Kms or so of largely barren coast on the Musandam peninsula is washed by the Arab Gulf. And yet Oman's minute, detached enclave at the tip of Musandam puts the strategically vital Strait of Hormuz within its territorial sea. This combination of being geographically outside the Gulf and being strategically essential to it gives Oman a unique place in the regional setting of the Gulf Co-operation Council and in the wider context of the industrialised world's access to the oil which passes through the Strait of Hormuz under Omani guardianship.

'In many other respects, too, Oman is in a class apart. Alone of Arab Gulf countries, it receives monsoon rainfall, contains mountain ranges rising over 3,000 meters, counts among its population large and very important non-Arab communities . . . has maintained over centuries a remarkable water-distribution system and associated agriculture, boasts relatively large, efficient and battle-hardened armed forces, has been fully independent and under the same ruling dynasty for over 200 years, and once controlled territory distant from the Gulf (Zanzibar and other parts of East Africa until 1856 and Gwadur, now in Pakistan, until 1958).'[1]

The country can be divided geographically into five main areas: the Musandam Peninsula and the mountainous range of the Hajar, the Batinah Coast, the area between the southern end of the mountain range and Dhofar, the Salalah plain, and finally the area merging into the Rub'al-Khali.

However, with the objective of enhancing social and economic development and improving the regional distribution of public services, His Majesty the Sultan issued Royal Decree No.6/91 (**Appendix I**) on 3rd February,

1991 approving the division of the country into eight administrative regions: Muscat, Al-Batinah, Musandam, A'Dhahirah, A'Dakhliyah, A'Sharqiyah, Al-Wusta and Dhofar.

According to the 1993 Census – the first ever – the population of the Sultanate was 2.02 million, with Omanis forming 74 per cent of the total population, the rest being expatriate workers and their families. **Chapter Annex Table 1.A.1** provides distribution of the population by region, *Wilayats* (districts within a region/governorate), number of families, Omanis and non-Omanis.

The various factors mentioned above coupled with traditional Omani hospitality and friendliness contribute to the magic that is Oman, and no one who has been to the country can fail to be moved by it.

1.2 Historical background

As mentioned in the Introduction, Oman is a land of antiquity – its history dates back to almost the third millennium BC. Since it is neither possible nor is it the intention of this study to cover the entire historical development of Oman, we shall concentrate here only on the period between 1932 and 1970, and this for two reasons. The first is that under the rule of Sultan Said bin Taimur (1932-70), Oman remained completely cut off from the rest of the world, and the majority of the population lived in a society akin to that of the Middle Ages with no general education, no health services, poor internal communications and repressive petty restrictions on personal freedom. The second reason is that 1970 marked the end of an era and the rebirth of Oman.

Sultan Said's first objective, upon succeeding his father in 1932, was to eliminate the debts he had inherited from him. Having achieved this, Said was determined that he was not going to fall into debt again:

> '. . . for we did not want to overburden the Sultanate's finances and weigh them down with new debts, after having paid off all the old ones. Doubtless it would have been easy to obtain money in various ways, but this could only have been by a loan with interest at a set percentage point. This amounts to usury, with which I completely disagree, and the religious prohibition of which is not unknown.'[2]

Sultan Said also pursued the principle that the only way to ensure that matters were handled properly was to handle them himself. Delegation was dangerous. Unfortunately, an adherence to these two principles almost brought life to a standstill. Although a small development department was set up in 1958, until 1967 the achievements were minimal: only 600 kms. of graded track (in a country whose total area exceeded 300,000 sq. kms.), suitable only for four-wheel drive vehicles; nine health centres inadequately staffed and equipped, with very few medicines and drugs; one primary school in Muttrah for boys; and two experimental farms. The policy of the Department during this period is outlined in an unpublished report by Ogram,[3] which states that the guiding principle was cautious development which would not damage the tradition of Oman.[4]

Education was a very low priority in the Sultan's development programme. In fact, the story of education during the Sultan's rule represents all the worst features of his attitudes and outlook. Out of an estimated population of 666,000, only 900 children were going to school in 1969.

Although oil was discovered in commercial quantities in Oman in 1964 and the first exports began in 1967 – we shall discuss the history of the discovery of oil and its impact on the creation of modern Oman in subsequent chapters – the Sultan continued his extremely cautious and perhaps reluctant policy towards development. The Word of Sultan Said bin Taimur,[5] Sultan of Muscat and Oman (as the country was known until its name was changed to Sultanate of Oman on 9th August, 1970 by a decision of HM Sultan Qaboos), about the history of the financial position of the Sultanate in the past and hopes for the future, after the export of oil reflects the unique form of Said's government, never previously experienced in Oman and the Arab World.

There was no way for the Omani people to make their voices heard by the Sultan. There was no formal or informal consultative assembly or council. As a result, an armed revolt started in Dhofar, southern Oman, in 1965, which was only extinguished by the new government of HM Sultan Qaboos bin Said on 2nd December, 1975, and in northern Oman many young men left the country illegally to seek education and employment.

For most of his reign, the Sultan had chosen to live an isolated existence in Dhofar. The only really effective means of consultation was by radio telephone and access to this was restricted to a select few. Petty restrictions abounded in the form of a curfew, bans on the import of vehicles unless personally approved by the Sultan and various other prohibitions, which might have the Sultan's approval but which could have no validity in an oil-producing state in the twentieth century. Even the Sultan's son and heir, Qaboos – who had been privately educated, initially in Salalah and later at Sandhurst – was under virtual house arrest and was not allowed to play any part in the affairs of the State.

On 23rd July, 1970 Said bin Taimur was deposed and signed a document of abdication in favour of his son Qaboos bin Said. Oman was reborn.

The legacy left by Sultan Said was a large underdeveloped country, with a population of about 666,000, three schools, 12 hospital beds, 10 kms. of paved roads, 557 telephone lines and a per capita income of less than US$400 (**Appendix Table VII.1**).

We will now review the processes and policies that were initiated with the assumption of power by HM Sultan Qaboos to achieve the socio-economic transformation of a stagnant, inefficient and underdeveloped economy within the constraints of poor initial conditions, inertia and an unstable external environment. We shall begin by analysing the development strategy that was adopted to deal with the dilemmas of a resource-based economy, and then examine the socio-economic changes that have taken place since 1970.

1   Pridham (ed.) (1987), Preface p.xiii.
2   Appendix II, The Word of Sultan Said bin Taimur (1968).
3   Ogram, Major DNR, Development Secretary, Oman (1962-67).
4   Clements (1980), p.58.
5   Appendix II, The Word of Sultan Said bin Taimur (1968).

Total Population by Regions and *Wilayats*: Omani and non-Omani (1993)

Region/ Governorate	Wilayat (district)	No. of Families	Population			Percentage of Omanis of total Population (%)
			Omani	Non-Omani	Total	
Muscat						
	Muscat	7,046	40,571	11,398	51,969	78
	A'Seeb	15,966	92,686	40,731	133,417	70
	Muttrah	46,888	93,015	168,308	261,323	36
	Bausher	14,052	45,519	62,740	108,259	42
	Al Amrat	4,371	30,015	6,163	36,178	83
	Quriyat	3,975	28,036	3,324	31,360	89
	Total	92,298	329,842	292,664	622,506	53
Al Batinah						
	Sohar	11,284	69,171	16,686	85,857	81
	A'Rustaq	7,004	53,138	6,241	59,379	90
	Shinas	5,287	36,189	6,344	42,533	85
	Liwa	2,672	18,781	2,682	21,463	88
	Saham	8,586	62,299	9,372	71,671	87
	Al Khabourah	5,108	33,440	4,989	38,429	87
	A'Suwaiq	10,204	69,629	11,536	81,165	86
	Nakhal	1,576	11,452	1,118	12,570	91
	Wadi Al Ma'awil	1,340	9,620	1,010	10,630	91
	Al Awabi	1,052	7,787	701	8,488	92
	Al Masna'ah	5,762	39,395	6,019	45,414	87
	Barka	8,498	47,183	13,981	61,164	77
	Total	68,373	458,084	80,679	538,763	85
Musandam						
	Khasab	2,254	12,714	3,041	15,755	81
	Bukha	519	2,794	1,073	3,867	72
	Diba Al-Bayah	949	4,443	1,140	5,583	80
	Madha	305	2,046	418	2,464	83
	Total	4,027	21,997	5,672	27,669	80
A'Dhahirah						
	Al Buraimi	6,150	28,673	17,484	46,157	62
	Ibri	9,996	72,397	15,917	88,214	82
	Mahadha	1,321	4,671	3,050	7,721	61
	Yanqul	1,955	12,325	1,833	14,158	87
	Dhank	1,748	11,677	1,683	13,360	87
	Total	21,170	129,743	39,967	169,610	76
A'Dakhliyah						
	Nizwa	6,990	47,725	8,502	56,227	85
	Samail	4,488	32,980	3,489	436,469	91
	Bahla	5,601	40,353	4,451	44,804	90
	Adam	1,881	10,864	2,374	13,238	82
	Al Hamra	1,566	12,804	894	13,698	94
	Manah	1,295	9,118	970	10,088	90
	Izki	3,445	25,220	3,411	28,631	88
	Bib Bid	2,045	14,938	2,310	17,248	87
	Total	27,311	194,002	26,401	220,403	88

Region/ Governorate	Wilayat	No. of Families	Population			Percentage of Omanis of total Population (%)
			Omani	Non-Omani	Total	
A'Sharqiyah						
	Sur	6,800	42,488	9,031	51,519	83
	Ibra	2,767	14,946	3,891	18,837	79
	Biddiya	2,566	12,383	2,052	14,435	86
	Al Qabil	1,961	10,035	1,345	11,380	88
	Al Mudhaibi	6,718	43,129	5,437	48,566	89
	Dima Wa A'Tayeen	1,837	12,810	1,009	13,819	93
	Al Kamil Wa Al Wafi	2,498	13,451	2,546	15,997	84
	Jalan Bani Bu Ali	5,575	33,307	4,124	37,431	89
	Jalan Bani Bu Hassan	2,900	17,081	2,325	19,406	88
	Wadi Bani Khalid	925	5,551	411	5,962	93
	Masirah	1,006	5,978	1,857	7,835	76
	Other Settlements	390	2,349	15	2,364	99
	Total	35,943	213,508	34,043	247,551	85
Al Wusta						
	Haima	260	1,466	749	2,215	66
	Muhut	1,187	7,011	482	7,493	94
	A'Duqm	521	2,760	496	3,256	85
	Al Jazer	416	1,967	1,170	3,137	63
	Total	2,384	13,204	2,897	16,101	82
Dhofar						
	Salalah	15,510	77,738	44,015	121,753	64
	Thumrait	1,428	4,085	2,652	6,737	61
	Taqah	1,768	12,736	2,056	14,792	86
	Mirbat	1,439	8,891	1,358	10,249	87
	Sadah	500	3,484	687	4,171	84
	Rakhyut	526	3,244	598	3,842	84
	Dhalkut	345	2,043	438	2,481	82
	Muqshin	103	360	170	530	68
	Al Halaniyat Islands	606	3,725	2,133	5,858	64
	Other Settlements	626	3,845	630	4,475	86
	Total	22,851	120,151	54,737	174,888	69
Total Population of the Sultanate of Oman		274,357	1,480,531	537,060	2,017,591	74

Source: Oman, *Preliminary Results of the General Census of Population, Housing and Establishments*, December 1993, pp.7-10.

Chapter Two

Dilemmas of a Resource-Based Development

A country's potential for economic growth, as Todaro[1] rightly points out, is greatly influenced by its physical resource endowment (its land, minerals, and other raw materials) and by its endowment of human resources (i.e. both the number of people and their level of skills).

However, given the scarcity of resources in developing countries in relation to development needs, one of the central issues in development economics is the allocation of resources among competing ends. A common starting-point in the consideration of resource allocation (e.g. the proportion for consumption in Oman itself, and at what price, and the proportion for export) is how to maximise the level or growth of output from the domestic resources available, and how to maximise foreign exchange to meet the import requirements of development.

Associated with these issues is the particular development strategy to be adopted. On the one hand, the classical growth theories emphasise the need to liberalise trade as a means of enlarging the market (Adam Smith) and permitting the exploitation of comparative advantage (Ricardo).[2] On the other hand, the structuralists led by Prebisch[3] have attacked the theory of comparative advantage as not fitting real life.

Oman, in fact, adopted a middle ground along the lines articulated by Rosenstein, Rodan and Nurkse,[4] i.e. it adopted the principle of comparative advantage to maximise resources from its primary commodity – oil – and carried out a massive investment programme, by using those resources, to achieve a process of economic expansion and structural diversification, as we shall see in Chapter Three.

In this chapter, we shall begin by reviewing the policies adopted for handling the multinationals and their role in the discovery of oil in Oman. Next we shall examine the dilemmas faced by a resource-based economy in dealing with questions of resource development and allocation, international terms of trade, external price instability and uncertainty. And then we shall review the strategies and policies adopted.

2.1 Oil and the multinationals

Until the early 1970s, almost 61 per cent[5] of the world's crude oil output was in the hands of the seven largest oil multinationals, known as the 'seven sisters' (Shell, Exxon, Mobil, Gulf, Standard Oil, Texaco and BP). The ability to control oil production meant that they were able to collude in setting the price of oil and, therefore, could exercise what has become recognised as a classic case of 'oligopolistic' power.

In the Gulf, the 'seven sisters', by achieving a collaborative strategy as opposed to operating in a free market competitive situation, were able greatly to reduce their production costs and to raise the returns achieved relative to each well that was drilled. There was not only collusion over the market price of oil but also over the strategy for oil exploration and production.

In fact most development economists, such as Streeten, Lall, Vaitsos,[6] saw these large multinationals, not in the neo-classical position of mutual wariness among firms in an oligopoly, but as acting in collusion precisely to remove competition and make life easier for themselves. There is no question of their seeking to allocate resources more efficiently, as the 'neo-classical' approach argues. As a result, multinationals are themselves instrumental in creating the market imperfections that characterise developing countries.

More recent commentators who adopt neo-imperialist[7] perspectives have seen multinationals as perpetuating underdevelopment through the draining of surpluses from the underdeveloped countries to the advanced capitalist countries.

A major consequence of the prevailing attitudes in the early 1970s was the promotion of policies of nationalisation of strategic resources, and of greater state control over multinationals in general. However, despite this trend and the nationalisation of the oil industry by a number of oil producing countries, Oman examined the various alternatives and decided to take only a 60 per cent share in PDO – the only company producing oil at that time – leaving the remaining 40 per cent to foreign shareholders. This approach was in line with the neo-classical and neo-fundamentalist interpretations of multinationals and their role in the economic development of Third World countries.[8] It was based on the assumption that foreign capital was complementary to local capital rather than displacing it, and that increasing competition between multinationals from different origins has increased the bargaining power of Third World countries. In fact, the retention of foreign shareholders provided Oman not only with the latest state-of-the-art technology, but with a sharing of risks, foreign capital, management expertise and the comfort that all new investments were subject to a thorough cost/benefit analysis.

As mentioned in the previous chapter, the country was almost on the brink of collapse when HM Qaboos bin Said took over. The legacy left by Said has been explained in the previous chapter. In fact the press release issued by HM Qaboos on 26th July, 1970 (**Appendix III**) reflects clearly the situation prevailing at that time.

We shall now review briefly the policies and the processes that have been instrumental in developing Oman's oil resources within the context of the international environment and the emergence of multinationals of contrasting origins (Japan, North America, Europe) in competition with each other.

2.2   Some perspectives on earlier developments

2.2.1 Discovery of oil in northern Oman

The story of oil in Oman extends over a period of time beginning with geological surveys in 1925. Production did not start until 1962 and the first exports were not until 1967. It is therefore a complex journey, in both technical and political terms, as all these developments took place during one of the most troubled periods in the Sultanate's history.

The first oil concession was granted in 1925, by the then Sultan, Taimur bin Faisal, to the d'Arcy Exploration Company, which was part of the Anglo Persian Oil Company. However, the licence was allowed to lapse after two years because of disappointing results.

A new concession was granted in 1937 to the Iraq Petroleum Company. Exploration was, however, interrupted by the Second World War and after some exploration activity following the war, the concession for Dhofar was relinquished in 1951; that for northern Oman was retained. By 1953 the company had adopted the name Petroleum Development (Oman) Ltd (PDO).

The disappointing exploration results and the glut of oil in the latter part of the decade caused all of the companies participating in PDO except Shell and Partex to withdraw in 1960. The two remaining companies held respectively 85 per cent and 15 per cent of the equity, though Compagnie Francaise de Petrole regained an interest through the purchase of 10 per cent of the Partex share in 1967.

Hard work and patience finally paid off and oil was discovered in commercial quantities in northern Oman – in Jibal in 1962, in Natih in 1963, and in Fahud in 1964. An announcement of the discovery of oil in commercial quantities was made in November 1964 with the prediction that exports would start in summer of 1967 at the rate of 140,000 barrels per day (b/d). Since oil had been discovered in central Oman a 30-inch pipeline to cover a distance of 173 miles to the coast was laid.

More commercially exploitable oil fields were found throughout the initial period and exports of crude oil rose from 20.9 million barrels in 1967 to 121.3 million barrels in 1970. We shall elaborate on this point later on in this chapter.

2.2.2 Oil development in southern Oman

Oil development in southern Oman has followed a different course to that of northern Oman. For, although Dhofar was included in the original concession granted in 1937, it was relinquished in 1951 on the establishment of PDO. The concession was granted by Sultan Said to Wendell Phillips the following year, who in turn transferred it to Dhofar Cities Services Petroleum Company – a subsidiary of Cities Service Company. Various partners were brought into the venture but, due to the prevailing low oil prices and the low production potential of oil discovered in the Marmul field, the venture was abandoned in 1967.

Exploration was revitalised in 1969 when an agreement was reached between the Sultan and PDO to bring the southern area back into the concessional area. The exploration activity was intensified and although oil was discovered in large quantities in the area in the early 1970s, it was not until 1977, when a new agreement was signed between His Majesty's government and PDO's private shareholders, that development of the southern oil fields began.

2.2.3 Offshore oil development

In December 1965 Wintershall A.G. was awarded a concession in Oman's economic waters, extending along Oman's north-east coast for a distance of 300 miles and into waters with a depth of 1,000 feet. In 1967, part of the concession relinquished by PDO in the territorial waters was added to the area awarded in 1965. However, despite intensive exploration in the offshore areas, results to date have been far from conclusive.

2.2.4 Oman's oil policy within the context of OPEC agreements

Although Oman is not a member of OPEC – formed in 1960 by a number of oil producing countries to co-ordinate their efforts in dealing with the oil multinationals, the so-called 'seven sisters' – it has always managed to apply the agreements reached within OPEC, to the extent that they were beneficial to Omani national interests, in its dealings with the oil companies operating within the Sultanate. Therefore, in accordance with OPEC, the agreement between the Sultan and PDO was amended in 1967 to give the government 50 per cent of the oil profits, and the right to 12.5 per cent of all oil exported. These events are well documented in The Word of Sultan Said (**Appendix II**).

During the early 1970s, the relationship between His Majesty's government and PDO underwent a further change, following the agreement reached in 1972 between OPEC and the 'seven sisters', which gave every oil-producing country a 25 per cent stake in all oil concessions, scheduled to rise to 51 per cent by 1982.[9] Accordingly, the Government acquired in early 1974 a holding of 25 per cent in PDO.

However, since the 1972 OPEC agreements were soon overtaken by events such as the nationalisation of oil production in Iraq in 1972,[10] rapidly followed by Kuwait, Qatar and Iran taking complete control of their oil industries, the agreement reached between the government and PDO's shareholders in 1973 was altered by mutual agreement to give the government a 60 per cent undivided interest in all of PDO's assets, liabilities and concessions with retroactive effect from 1 January 1974. A Joint Management Committee was established to implement the new participation agreement (**Appendix IV**).

2.3 Oil strategy

Any analysis of the development of oil involves an examination of the strategies adopted in dealing with the questions of resource development and allocation, international terms of trade and external price instability. However, before we examine these interrelated issues, we will briefly mention the processes which provided the dynamics for the development of the oil sector and its integration into the national economy:

a The takeover of decision-making was a crucial development. By virtue of the agreement reached in late 1973, which was subsequently amended, for the government to acquire a 60 per cent interest in PDO and the formation of a Joint Management Committee w.e.f. 1 January 1974, the government was able for the first time to influence – to the extent possible – the exploration and production activities of PDO.

b The increase in the price of oil in 1974 and 1979 – a point we shall discuss later – made a lot of oil fields commercially viable for the first time, especially the southern oil fields, which were considered at the time to be of inferior quality and in insufficient quantity to justify commercial exploitation.

c The agreement signed in May 1977 between the government and the foreign partners of PDO, which was designed to provide an incentive to the foreign partners to develop the southern oil fields. The agreement had three main elements: an accelerated depreciation of the foreign partners' assets – all investment was to be depreciated at 40 per cent in the first year, 30 per cent in the second year and 10 per cent in each of the next three years; a guaranteed income for the foreign partners, net of operation costs and depreciation, of US$0.23 a barrel on all oil produced, indexed to the buy-back price of Omani crude; and a return of 7.5 per cent on their share of PDO's average assets.

d Increasing oil revenues enabled the government to meet its twin objectives of increasing the oil reserves and enhancing production levels. Investments in the oil sector were increased substantially. Investment in the oil sector which stood at RO 402 million during the First FYP (1976–80) increased to RO 1,034 million in the Second FYP (1981-85), i.e. an increase of almost 160 per cent.[11]

e The continued growth in the demand for oil on the one hand, and the growing competition between a rising number of multinationals – referred to by Warren as one of the factors enabling capitalist development in the Third World[12] – enabled the government during the second half of the 1970s to revive the interest of international oil companies in obtaining concessions and exploring for oil in Oman. **Chapter Annex Table 2.A.1** shows companies operating in Oman as at 1 January 1993.

2.3.1 Oil development and the staple theory of growth

An overriding issue in the relations between trade and development is the ultimate question of whether there is a conflict between the gains from trade and the gains from growth. Are the dictates of comparative advantage incompatible with the requirements of accelerated development?

The orthodox interpretation as expounded by classical and neo-classical economists is that foreign trade can be a propelling force in development. Adam Smith's model of foreign trade postulates the existence of idle land and labour before a country is opened to world markets. The excess resources are used to produce a surplus of goods for export, and trade thereby 'vents' a surplus productive capacity that would otherwise be unused.

The staple theory of growth also postulates that with the discovery of a primary product in which the country has a comparative advantage, or with an increase in the demand for its comparative advantage commodity, there is an expansion of a resource-based export commodity; this in turn, induces higher rates of growth of aggregate and per capita income. Previously idle or undiscovered resources are brought into use, creating a return to these resources – consistent with venting a surplus through trade.[13]

The strategy adopted for development from 1976 onwards by the government and embodied in the successive Five-Year Plans was in fact very much in line with the neo-classical theory of trade and development. By using oil as a leading sector, the government used all its efforts to optimise oil production and reserves and maximise exports of oil by minimising domestic consumption. This policy was based, as Prebisch[14] and other structuralists also emphasised, on the premise that increased self-sufficiency in the long term requires, as a precondition, increased imports and, hence increased access to foreign exchange.

2.3.2 Oil resources development: reserves and production

Oil reserves comprise the stock of oil believed to be potentially available in the oil-bearing rocks of a country, while only a fraction of those reserves extracted in any one year will enter into the statistics of annual oil production. The dilemma that a country with a depleting resource is always faced with is whether to extract its oil as rapidly as possible or to make it last longer.

In the early years of Oman's Renaissance, the government's policy was directed towards maximising oil output in order to meet the basic requirements of a modern state. This was dictated not only by the state of stagnation the country was in, but by the limited size of its proven reserves, which stood at about 1.8 billion barrels in 1973.

The main target and policies of the First FYP (1976-80), as far as oil was concerned, was to arrest the decline of production levels and increase the level of reserves. Although oil production did decline from about 134 million barrels in 1976 to about 102 million barrels in 1980 (**Chapter Annex Table 2.A.2**), the following years witnessed a gradual and sustained increase in production.

At the same time, oil reserves in the PDO concession area (PDO was the only producing company in Oman until 1980), which had declined to 1,280 million barrels in 1976 – equal to about 10 years of the then production level – had increased to 2,484 million barrels by the end of 1980 – equal to almost 24 years at the prevailing production level (**Chart 2.1**).

Another important factor in the development of the oil sector was the agreement reached with the foreign shareholders of PDO in March 1986 whereby it was agreed that effective from 1 January 1986 the government would pay the private shareholders of PDO a fee, net of Omani income-tax, of 40 US cents per barrel of the increase of the Expected Ultimate Recovery in each year.

The logic of this agreement was to provide an added incentive to the foreign shareholders to make experience, technology and know-how available so that PDO could conduct an intensive program of exploration and appraisal/appreciation of oil reserves, in order to meet the government's aim of increasing the oil reserves of PDO, in particular through exploration, and thus to increase the Expected Ultimate Recovery.

The oil sector strategy outlined in the Fourth FYP lays down very clearly the government's oil policy on oil reserves and production:

> Conserve and increase the oil reserves as much as possible, commensurate with the targeted production rates, through exploration, reassessment of fields, intensive study of the oil areas, development of exploration and methods of extraction. In this context it is aimed to increase oil reserves by 237 million barrels annually to meet the targeted levels of Production.[15]

Table 2.1 below demonstrates clearly the success of the oil strategy. Oil production increased by about 96 per cent between the period 1976-80 and 1986-90, leading to the almost doubling of oil revenues, which increased from RO 3,125 million during 1976-80 to RO 6,016 million during 1986-90. At the same time, and despite the increased level of production, the average life of oil reserves has increased from about 10 years in 1976 to 17 years in 1990 (**Chart 2.1**).

Table 2.1
Growth of Oil Production and Revenues (1976-90)

	1976-80	1981-85	1986-90
Oil Production (Million Barrels)	574	719	1,127
Index	100	125	196
Oil Revenues (Million RO)	3,125	6,649	6,016
Index	100	213	193

Source: Oman, Ministry of Development data; Oman, Ministry of Petroleum and Minerals data.

Chart 2.1
Annual Production of Oil (1967-93)

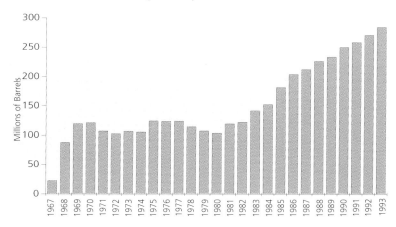

Oil Reserves (1967-93)

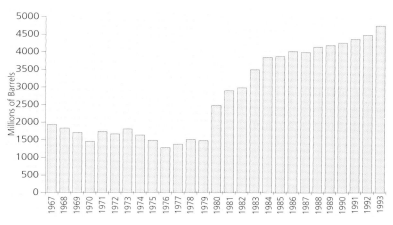

Life of Oil Reserves (1967-93)

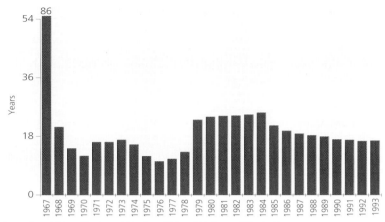

Source : Oman, Ministry of Development data; Oman, Ministry of Petroleum and Minerals data.

It is worth mentioning that although PDO is the main oil producer, three other oil companies, namely ELF, OXY and Japex, produced between 6 and 8 per cent of Omani oil between 1990 and 1992 (**Chapter Annex Table 2.A.3**).

In order to achieve its objective of maximising oil reserves, optimising production and treating oil as the leading sector, the government has been instrumental in directing an increasing amount of investment – both private and public – towards the development of the oil sector. Whilst the percentage of investments allocated to the oil sector (gross fixed capital formation) during 1976-85 amounted to an annual average of about 20 per cent of GDP, this percentage increased to 29.3 per cent during 1986-90 and jumped to 33.4 per cent during 1991-92 (**Appendix Table VII.2**).

2.3.3 Resource allocation

Central to the issue of resource allocation is the choice between present and future consumption which is the same as the choice between consumption and investment at present. Therefore, policy makers in an oil producing country have to determine *interalia*:

– What balance to strike between domestic consumption of oil and export?

– At what rate should oil be priced for domestic consumption?

Both questions are in fact interrelated. If the domestic price is set low,

35

demand will continue to increase and hence the quantities available for export will decline, thus affecting resources available for investment in terms of government revenues and the country's foreign exchange earnings. On the other hand, if prices are set higher than prevailing international prices – opportunity cost – they will affect the competitiveness of the local industry.

The government's policy in this regard was clearly laid down in the Second FYP (1981-85) which stated:

> 'To aim at exporting the crude oil produced except for the amounts required for the refinery (planned to start production in mid 1982). Therefore, the recourse to crude oil or to oil products for power generation will be minimised, and natural gas will replace it for those purposes wherever it is economically justified.'[16]

This policy, in sharp contrast to the prevailing trend in most oil exporting countries to sell oil for domestic consumption at almost subsidised prices, was in fact, influenced to a great extent by the relatively low levels of both per capita and per sq. kms. oil reserves and production in Oman, as compared to other Gulf Co-operation Council countries (**Chart 2.2**).

As a result of this conservative and perhaps wise policy and as **Chart 2.3** shows, virtually all of Oman's oil was exported prior to 1982. Since then, with the coming on stream of the domestic refinery, part of the oil, ranging from 8 to 10 million barrels a year, or about 3 to 4 per cent of total production, has been consumed domestically.

The importance of appropriate pricing policies was also highlighted in the communiqué issued at the end of the Fifth Arab Energy Conference, held in Cairo, Egypt, on 7-10 May 1994, which states, *interalia*, under Energy Demand and Energy Pricing:

> 'The Conference noted that energy pricing policies in the domestic markets of the Arab countries vary markedly according to the availability of energy sources in a particular country. In some Arab countries domestic energy prices exceed the world levels, while in other Arab countries they are much lower. Believing that the significance and impact of domestic energy pricing policies will increase in future, the Conference stressed the importance of according more attention to this issue and undertaking further studies to enable domestic pricing policies to play a constructive role in the development process.'[17]

Chart 2.2

Oil Production per Capita: Oman vs. Selected Countries (1993)

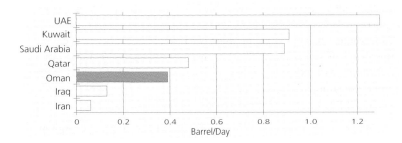

Oil Production in Proportion to Area of National Territory: Oman vs. Selected Countries (1993)

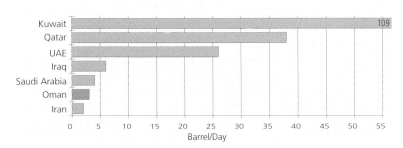

Population Density by Country: Oman vs. Selected Countries (1993)

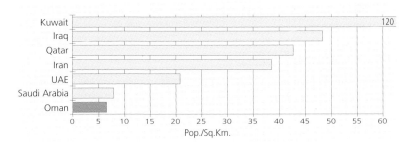

Oil Reserves: Oman vs. Selected Countries (1993)

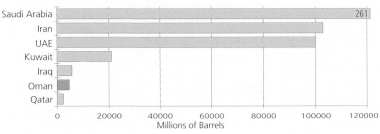

Sources : Area and Population : *International Country Risk Guide* (1994); Production of Oil : OPEC, *OPEC at a Glance* (1993);
BP Statistical Review of World Energy June1994; (Iraq Oil Production, 1989 data).

Chart 2.3
Crude Petroleum: Production and Exports (1970-92)

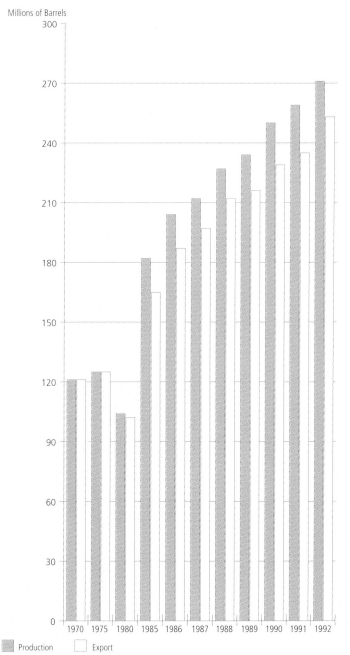

Source: Oman, *Statistical Year Book 1993*, p.195.

The government policy to minimise domestic consumption and hence free the available resources for export has been achieved through:

a A pricing mechanism, which has been in place since 1982, whereby half of the crude oil supplied to the refinery – i.e. the quantity estimated for domestic consumption – is priced at US$30 per barrel, almost twice its 1994 international price, while the other half – the estimated residue oil which the refinery exports – is priced at the prevailing international price. The price charged for domestic consumption is not only intended to encourage efficient use but also to provide an additional source of government revenue.

b The development of natural gas as an alternative source of energy, whereby most of the fuel required for power generation is met by natural gas. It is important to mention that up to now natural gas is priced almost at twice its international price, i.e. at US$2.08 per cubic foot. The pricing of natural gas is also based on the same principle of conservation and efficiency.

The success of the government's policy in maximising exports and minimising domestic consumption is illustrated by **Chart 2.3**, which shows that despite the growth of industrial activity and the continuous increase in population, only about 3 to 4 per cent of total oil production is consumed domestically, with the balance being exported.

2.4 Oil and international terms of trade

One of the main criticisms made by the structuralist school against the theory of comparative advantage is that, while manufacturing nations have retained the benefits of their own productivity gains, the extent of the movement in the terms of trade suggest that they have also absorbed part of the productivity gains of primary exports (which were passed on through a decline in relative prices, as the theory of comparative advantage would predict).[18]

We will, therefore, analyse hereunder the problems of dependence on the export of a single primary product and the impact of oil price instability on the development process.

2.4.1 Who controls oil ?

Oil sales revenue is made up of two components. One is income generated from international oil sales; this portion of oil income is indeed very important for a country like Oman, where oil sales represent about 90 per cent of foreign exchange earnings; hence the importance of minimising domestic consumption and maximising exports. The other component is made up of sales for domestic consumption. Oil sales revenue, therefore, depends on the volume of oil production, the level of exports and domestic consumption, international oil prices and domestic consumption prices.

Whilst the government policy – as we have seen earlier – can influence the volume of production, the level of exports and the volume and price of oil consumed domestically, the export price of oil is decided exogenously. As Findlay[19] points out, spatial control, in the sense of oil reserves being located

Chart 2.4

Who Controls Oil ?

A Schematic Representation of the World Oil Industry

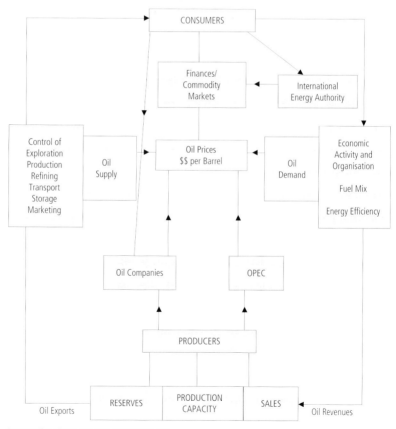

Source: Findlay, Allan M., *The Arab World* (1994), p.76.

Chart 2.5
Fluctuations in the International Price of Oil (1972-91)

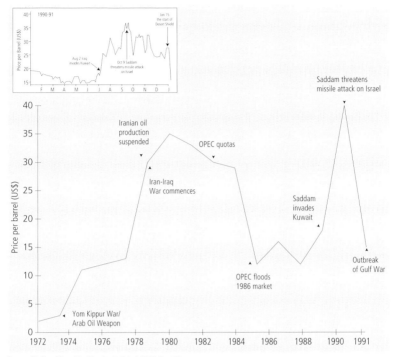

Source: Findlay, Allan, M., *The Arab World* (1994), p.82.

within the state boundaries of a country, does not ensure that a producer country gets maximum benefit from oil sales. Of much greater significance are the intervening actors in the world oil trade. **Chart 2.4** shows that many other actors in the oil industry have intervened over the years in their own interests, relative to trends in oil prices and supply.

The relative power of these different actors has changed through time, both in relation to each other and to the varying demand for oil. Perhaps the most reliable indicator of who controls oil at any one time is the oil price, as shown in **Chart 2.5**.

One of the most remarkable feature of **Chart 2.5** is that it tells us that the trend of oil prices is unpredictable.

2.4.2 Terms of trade

Central to the issue of comparative advantage and international trade is the question of terms of trade. Since the early twentieth century, primary producing countries have fared poorly in international trading relations. In

41

fact, between 1954 and 1962, the terms of trade between primary commodities (including oil) and manufactured products deteriorated by between 10 and 15 per cent. This happened at a time when 70 to 90 per cent of exports of virtually all developing countries were primary commodities and 50 to 60 per cent of imports were manufactured goods. Terms of trade for non-oil producing countries have become even worse since the early 1970s.[20] Oil producers seemed to have bucked the trend, but even for them prices have fallen dramatically in both current and real terms since the early 1980s. **Chart 2.6** below demonstrates the steep decline in Oman's oil prices since the early 1980s.

Chart 2.6
Oil Prices (1973-94)

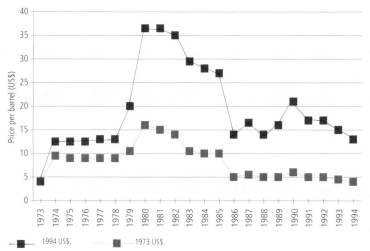

Source: Oman, Ministry of Petroleum and Minerals data.

The structuralist attack on the theory of comparative advantage was linked to the empirical observation that, contrary to the theory's prediction, the benefits of technological advance in primary exporting and manufacturing economies are not equitably distributed between the two trading partners. Prebisch (1964) emphasises the further depressing effects on demand for primary exports from the periphery of growing protectionism in European agriculture, and increased efficiency in the industrial economies in the use of raw materials, leading to less input per unit of output.[21]

The gradual decline of oil prices since the 1980s bears out Prebisch's analysis. Due to economies made in energy consumption in industrialised countries, world energy use, which had been growing at 4.9 per cent per annum in the post-war period prior to 1973, witnessed slackening of demand after the oil price increase, and during the next decade grew at only 2 per cent per annum. Similarly, the development of alternative fuels resulted in oil accounting for only 44.6 per cent of world energy demand in 1987 compared with 53.4 per cent in 1979.[22]

Although Oman, being an oil producing country, benefited from oil price increases in 1974 and 1980, and its export price index increased from 62.0 in 1974 to 103.7 in 1992, the increase in its import price index was much steeper, jumping from 46.1 to 119.5 during the same period, thus offsetting all the gains accruing from oil price increases. As a result, its overall terms of trade index declined from 134.6 in 1974 (1987=100) to 86.8 in 1992.[23]

2.4.3 Policies dealing with oil price instability

With oil prices becoming increasingly unpredictable and subject to sharp fluctuations, all oil producing countries face the major dilemma of how to insulate the economy from the impact of international trade cycles on development. We shall, therefore, briefly examine the mechanism that the Omani government adopted in this regard from 1980 onwards. In fact, the policy response of the government to the question of imbalances was based on neo-classical monetarist solutions.

Initially the increased oil revenues from the oil price increase in 1974 to about US$11 per barrel from US$3 per barrel in 1973 were added to the government accounts, giving a much needed boost to an economy just emerging from the state of long stagnation to which we have referred earlier. In addition, increasing funds had to be allocated for the purpose of defence and national security, since the government was fighting an insurgency in southern Oman.

2.4.3.1. Establishment of the State General Reserve Fund

With the second oil price increase in 1979 and 1980, the government decided in 1980 to put a part of the additional revenues into a reserve, outside the budget, called the State General Reserve Fund (SGRF), established by Royal Decree No.1/80 (**Appendix V**) issued on 6 January 1980. Article Eight of the decree stipulated that 15 per cent of each sum received from oil revenues should be transferred to the Fund. In addition, all income from the investments of the SGRF assets was to be reinvested in the Fund. Article Six stipulated that there should be no withdrawals from the SGRF except for the purpose of financing a deficit in the state budget in the years which may require such withdrawals. **Chart 2.7** below indicates the proportion of oil revenue flowing into the SGRF from 1980 onwards.

Chart 2.7
Proportion of Gross Oil Revenues Flowing into the SGRF (1980-93)

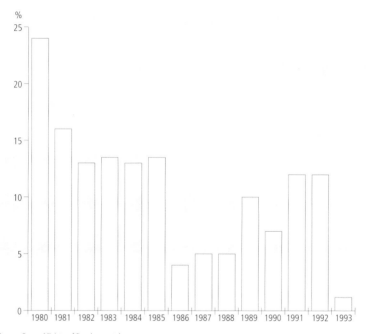

Source: Oman, Ministry of Development data.

The proportion of gross oil revenues flowing into the SGRF followed the trend of oil prices and oil revenues accruing to the government. In fact, the transfers into the SGRF reached almost 25 per cent in 1980, when the average price of oil increased to US $32.19 from US $20.07 per barrel, but these transfers declined in the mid eighties and plunged to 3.6 per cent in 1986 when the average oil price collapsed to almost half that of the prices achieved in 1985 (**Chapter Annex Table 2.A.4**).

The government's objective in setting up the SGRF was two-fold. The first objective was to provide a source of income for the future to be used – as per Article Six of the decree mentioned earlier – to finance the state budget in the years which may require such withdrawals. The second objective was to minimise the effects of the so-called 'Dutch disease'. Countries experiencing large windfalls such as improvements in their terms of trade through sharp increases in, say, the export prices of oil or gas, tend to be afflicted by 'Dutch disease' through market forces or frivolous fiscal, monetary and exchange-rate policies. Events like these create large income effects that tend to drive up the prices of non-traded goods and services, labour, and land (assuming free capital movement) that, because of market imperfections, may prevail after the reversal of the initial windfall or may lead to deficits in the public sector that may be politically irreversible. If windfalls were forever, there would be no special problems; however, they do not last.[24]

The SGRF did achieve its objective very effectively. Were it not for the SGRF, the economy would have almost collapsed in 1986 because of the drastic fall in the oil price. In that year, almost 30 per cent of the government expenditure was met from withdrawals from the SGRF[25] (**Chapter Annex Table 2.A.4**).

To offset further the adverse effects of the collapse of the oil price in 1986, the Omani Rial was devalued by 10 per cent and all current government expenditure was cut by 15 per cent while certain development projects were deferred.

To mitigate further the adverse effects of the oil price collapse, and since all indicators were pointing towards a prolonged period of low oil prices, the government intensified its efforts – to which we have referred earlier – to increase the level of oil production without seriously impairing the life of the oil reserves.

2.4.3.2 Establishment of the Contingency Fund

In formulating the Fourth FYP (1991-95) the following additional precautionary measures were incorporated in the plan (**Appendix VI**):

a The transfers to SGRF from oil revenue, which had been reduced to 5 per cent during the Third Five-Year Plan, were raised back to 15 per cent, as stated in Royal Decree No.1/80 which established the SGRF.

b A Contingency Fund was established to receive 7.5 per cent of the net oil revenues if oil prices ranged between US$18-20 per barrel, and 10 per cent if the price per barrel exceeded US$20 and up to US$22. Its purpose was to provide an initial source of funding for the public sector deficit and thus obviate ad hoc recourse to the SGRF, which would revert to being a more strategic, long-term reserve. **Chart 2.8** below shows the overall structure of the Government's financial stocks and flows following the establishment of the Contingency Fund.

Chart 2.8

Simplified Structure of Financial Stocks and Flows

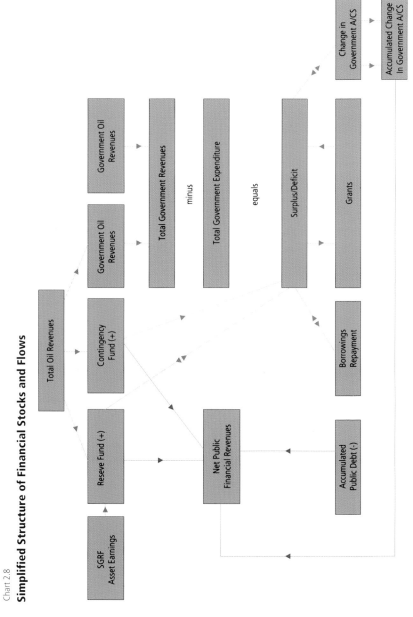

2.4.3.3 Fiscal measures

The Fourth FYP also provides for a review of expenditure to match any fall in oil revenues resulting from decline in international oil prices, so that the ratio of deficit between total revenue and total expenditure should not exceed 10 per cent of total revenue.

The revised mechanism adopted in the Fourth FYP to insulate the government oil revenues from fluctuations of oil prices was very effective during the first three years of the Fourth Plan (1991-93). As **Table 2.2** below illustrates, although the actual oil prices have been below budget, the revenues accruing to the treasury have stayed the same, with both SGRF and the Contingency Fund acting as stabilisers, especially in 1993. (The slight difference between actual revenue per barrel allocated to the Treasury and the planned allocation is due to production increases, so the total amount of dollars transferred remained the same.)

Table 2.2
Distribution of Oil Revenues (1991-93)

Details	Planned			Actual		
	1991	1992	1993	1991	1992	1993
Annual Production of Oil (Millions of Barrels)	251.85	247.47	248.93	258.87	268.71	282.92
Price Average per Barrel (US$)	18.0	19.0	20.0	18.1	17.9	16
Transferred to:						
SGRF per Barrel	2.3	2.4	2.6	2.3	2.3	0.2
Contingency Fund per Barrel	0.9	1.0	1.4	1.0	0.6	0.0
Revenue per Barrel Allocated for Public Expenditure	14.8	15.6	16.0	14.8	15.0	15.6

Source: Oman, Ministry of Development data.

2.5 Conclusion

We began this chapter with a review of the history of oil discovery in Oman and the policies that were adopted to deal with the dilemmas normally faced by a resource-based development – as in the case of Oman.

We have seen that the government of the Sultanate of Oman, by adopting the principles of comparative advantage, has been successful in maximising the resources available for the socio-economic transformation of the country. In its dealing with the oil multinationals, and despite the prevailing negative attitudes of the 1970s towards them, we have seen that the government, by adopting the neo-classical perspective of multinationals and through appropriate policies, was able to draw upon its technical and financial resources to expand oil production and oil reserves. In fact, it is clear that the oil multinationals contributed almost 50 per cent of the total amount invested in the oil sector over the period 1976-92 (**Appendix Table VII.2**).

However, as we have demonstrated, the constraints on a more intensive transformation of the economy are due to deteriorating terms of trade for Oman, i.e. operation of the international political economy which makes an impact on Oman's domestic policy, rather than any weakness or lack of will embodied in this policy.

1   Todaro (1989), p.20.
2   Hunt (1989), p.34.
3   Ibid., p.320.
4   Ibid., pp.53-5.
5   Gwynne (1990), p.126.
6   Ibid., pp.118-30.
7   Ibid., p.127.
8   Ibid., p.130.
9   Findlay (1994), p.79.
10 Ibid.
11 Oman, *Third FYP* (1986), p.76.
12 Hunt (1989), pp.190-91.
13 Meier (1989), pp.381-84.
14 Hunt (1989), p.133.
15 Oman, *Fourth FYP* (1991), p.198.
16 Oman, *Second FYP* (1981), p. 59.
17 *Middle East Economic Survey* Vol. 37, No.35, (1994).
18 Hunt (1989), p.131.
19 Findlay (1994), p.76.
20 Gwynne (1990), pp.29-44.
21 Hunt (1989), pp.130-33.
22 Findlay (1994), p.81.
23 World Bank, *World Tables* (1989), p.510.
24 Hansen (1991), p.526.
25 Oman, *Third FYP* (1986), p.60.

Chapter Annex Table 2.A.1

Oil Concessions in Force on 1 January 1993

Company	Date of Agreement	Area (Sq. Km)	Site
Petroleum Development Oman (PDO)	1937-91	198,100	Various Onshore
	1987-91	16,051	Offshore
Amoco	Feb 1973	21,246	Masirah Gulf
	May 1981	48,900	Oman Mountains
	Apr 1988	—	South, Near Wahiba
	Dec 1988	14,050	Affar
Elf/Sumitomo/Wintershall	June 1992	4,033	Butabul
Occidental/Neste	Dec 1975	11,793	Sunainah
Occidental/Chevron/Quintana	May 1985	4,000	Near Abu Dhabi Border
Japex Oman	July 1981	4,400	Wadi Aswad
IPC/Tethys/BHP	Mar 1984	48,500	Batinah (Offshore)
IPC/Transworld Oil	Feb 1985	655	Bukha
IPC	May 1987	1,569	Ghubbali
Wintershall	Dec 1988	23,000	Saiwan
Conquest Exploration	July 1989	1,390	Jabel Aswad
Transworld Oil	Sep 1991	950	Affar
Transworld Oil	Mar 1992	50,000	Mainly Eastern Foothills

BHP, with a 60 per cent share, failed to find a partner to enter the fourth exploration period, which carried one commitment well, and hence relinquished its share in July 1992.

Source: Economist Intelligence Unit, *Country Profile: Oman, Yemen, 1993/94*, p.21.

Chapter Annex Table 2.A.2

Oil Extraction, Reserves, Life of Reserves and Exports (1967-93)

Years	Daily Extraction in 1,000's of Barrels	Annual Extraction in Millions of Barrels	Reserves in Millions of Barrels	Life of Reserves (Years)	Exports in Millions of Barrels
1967	57	22.5	1935	86.00	22
1968	241	87.9	1832	20.84	88
1969	328	119.7	1709	14.28	120
1970	332	121.3	1455	12.00	121
1971	294	107.4	1741	16.21	106
1972	282	102.8	1669	16.24	103
1973	293	107.0	1810	16.92	107
1974	290	105.8	1638	15.48	106
1975	341	124.6	1487	11.93	125
1976	366	133.8	1280	10.34	134
1977	340	124.2	1379	11.10	122
1978	314	114.7	1514	13.20	115
1979	295	107.7	2480	23.03	107
1980	282	103.7	2484	23.95	102
1981	328	119.8	2899	24.20	120
1982	336	122.6	2982	24.32	119
1983	389	141.9	3494	24.62	129
1984	416	152.4	3844	25.22	135
1985	498	181.8	3869	21.28	165
1986	560	204.3	4016	19.66	187
1987	582	212.5	3991	18.78	197
1988	619	226.6	4144	18.29	212
1989	641	233.8	4187	17.91	216
1990	695	250.1	4256	17.02	229
1991	708	258.2	4363	16.88	235
1992	742	270.8	4474	16.52	253
1993	780	284.6	4736	16.64	267

Source: Oman, *Statistical Year Books.*

Chapter Annex Table 2.A.3

Main Indicators of the Petroleum Sector (1990-92)

Items	1990	1991	1992
Producing Companies			
PDO			
Production	238.1	242.6	253.4
Export	221.1	223.7	239.6
Capital Formation	206.7	239.2	586.4
Wages and Salaries	58,344	56,297	59,978
Employees	4,737	4,765	4,857
ELF			
Production	1.9	3.4	4.7
Export	2.0	3.0	5.0
Capital Formation	8.4	9.4	5.3
Wages and Salaries	100	100	883
Employees	58	58	51
OXY			
Production	8.7	9.5	9.8
Export	4.7	5.0	5.1
Capital Formation	12.2	7.8	4.8
Wages and Salaries	2,114	2,530	1,786
Employees	55	84	84
JAPEX			
Production	1.4	3.0	2.9
Export	1.5	3.0	2.8
Capital Formation	9.7	9.7	2.7
Wages and Salaries	51	204	1,137
Employees	24	34	840
GRAND TOTAL			
Production	250.1	258.5	270.8
Export	229.3	234.7	252.5
Capital Formation	237	266.1	599.2
Wages and Salaries	60,609	59,131	63,784
Employees	4,874	4,941	5,032
***Concessionary companies**			
Capital Formation	10	4.4	13.7

Key: Production and Export - Million Barrels
     Capital Formation - Million RO   Wages and Salaries - Thousand RO   Employees - Number
     *Companies that have not yet reached production stage

Source: Oman, *Statistical Year Book 1992*, p.201.

Chapter Annex Table 2.A.4

Oil Revenues, State General Reserve Fund and Contingency Fund (1980-93)

Year	Oil Revenue (Million RO)	State General Reserve Fund (Million RO)	%	Contingency Fund (Million RO)	Withdrawal from State General Reserve Fund (Million RO)
1980	1095.5	264.3	24.1		
1981	1341.3	215.9	16.1		
1982	1215.7	158.4	13.0		
1983	1277.5	169.9	13.3		80.0
1984	1304.6	172.5	13.2		145.0
1985	1510.0	203.2	13.5		300.0
1986	928.9	33.9	3.7		526.4
1987	1194.9	51.9	4.3		198.4
1988	993.6	42.8	4.3		274.6
1989	1197.4	113.0	9.4		254.9
1990	1701.6	113.6	6.7	50.0	0.0
1991	1515.7	193.0	12.7	52.0	50.0
1992	1525.1	195.2	12.8	54.1	234.2
1993	1331.6	16.3	1.2	0.6	658.1

Source: Oman, Ministry of Development data.

Chapter Three

The Role of Oil in the Growth and Structural Transformation of the Economy

Planning in a variety of forms is frequently advocated as an alternative to the market mechanism and the use of market prices for the allocation of resources in developing countries. Reliance on the market mechanism and market prices for resource allocation is criticised on several grounds. Firstly, given people's natural preference for present rather than future satisfaction, resources in a free market will tend to be allocated for the production of goods for immediate consumption rather than for building the means of production, i.e. for production of capital goods. Secondly, market prices may provide a very imperfect guide to the social optimum allocation of resources, because they do not reflect the opportunity cost or value to society of the use of factors of production or the production of certain commodities. Thirdly, because of external factors, many projects that developing countries need, and that would be profitable to society, may not appear profitable under a pure market system, in which all investment decisions are left to private individuals. The level of investment may fall below the social optimum, firstly because private investors ignore external economies and the supplementary benefits of projects when calculating prospective returns, and secondly because the element of risk will be higher for a series of unco-ordinated individual projects than for co-ordinated investment programmes systematically undertaken with some central direction.[1]

For a variety of reasons, therefore, interference with the market mechanism is seen by some as a necessary prerequisite for a more rapid pace of development. However, whatever form the interference with the market mechanism takes, it will inevitably involve some degree of state intervention and control over means of production, distribution, exchange, and partial replacement of the market mechanism.

A clear statement of this viewpoint was presented in a 1965 report of a UN conference on planning, which asserted:

> 'It is an integral task of planning to achieve the best possible use of scarce resources for economic development . . . The need for using appropriate criteria for selecting projects arose because of the failure of the market mechanism to provide a proper guideline. In less-developed economies, market prices of such factors of production as labour, capital and foreign exchange deviated substantially from their social opportunity costs and were not, therefore, a correct measure of the relative scarcity or abundance of the factor in question.'[2]

On the other hand, whatever a country's political ideology, a development plan is an ideal way for a government to set out its development objectives and to demonstrate initiative in tackling the country's development problems. A development plan can serve as a stimulant to effort throughout the country, and also act as a catalyst for foreign investment and agency capital from international institutions.

Although Rostow in his book, *The Stages of Economic Growth: A Non Communist Manifesto*, considered that most societies emerged from the traditional stage (one of the five stages of development: traditional, transitional, take-off, maturity and high mass consumption) some time ago, Oman in 1970, mainly under the impact of external challenge and aggression or nationalism, and as described in Chapter One, was still an almost traditional society with a very high proportion of the work-force employed in agriculture and very little mobility or social change.[3]

What made development planning a necessity, therefore, rather than a convenience, was, in addition to the several reasons cited above, the state of stagnation the country was in and the necessity for the state to take a leading role in the structural transformation of the country through a rational and strategic allocation of investible resources. The urgent need to initiate the development process was reinforced by the fact that Oman's oil reserves and production capacity - as explained earlier - were very limited, and by the government's acknowledgement that oil wealth was a depleting resource. Every effort was needed for Oman to move - in the Rostowian definition - from the traditional stage to the take-off stage, by directing an increasing amount of resources towards income-producing investments.

We shall, therefore, now examine the development strategy adopted for achieving growth and economic diversification, the factors that contributed to the outcome, and the role of oil in achieving the twin objectives.

3.1 Long-term development strategy

The long-term development strategy adopted by the Development Council of Oman on 9 February 1975 fully reflected the above concerns, which were to be dealt with through development planning. This strategy can be summarised as follows:[4]

1 To develop new sources of national income to augment and eventually to replace oil revenues.

2 To increase the ratio of national investments directed to income-generating projects, particularly in manufacturing, mining, agriculture and fisheries.

3 To distribute national investments among geographical regions with a view to spreading prosperity and progress to all regions of the Sultanate, reducing differentials in the standard of living between the regions, and assigning a special priority to the least developed areas.

4 To support the maintenance of existing population centres and communities, to safeguard those communities from potential emigration to densely populated urban centres, and to protect the environment.

5 To attach high priority to the development of natural water resources as a vital prerequisite for continued economic activity and growth.

6 To attach high priority to the development of local human resources, and to improve their capability for contribution to the national economy.

7 To meet infrastructure requirements.

8 To support commercial activities by removing market deficiencies, particularly in the areas of transport, communications, storage and other obstacles to competitive trading, with a view to enhancing the emergence of a competitive market and maintaining a reasonable level of prices.

9 To provide for the creation of a national economy based on private enterprise and free from monopolistic practices. For this purpose the government is seen as extending to the private sector, to the degree permitted by the availability of resources, various incentives, tax exemptions, concessional loans, and to participate in the equity of vital projects.

10 To improve the efficiency of the government administration.

Central to Oman's development strategy was the paradoxical role of oil. On one hand, oil being the leading sector, i.e. the primary growth sector,[5] as defined by Rostow, which plays a key role both during the take-off and subsequently – the government's oil strategy[6] – as discussed in Chapter Two, was to maximise oil revenues through effective resource development and allocation policies, and thus use the resources made available for propelling the rest of the economy. On the other hand, the first objective of the development strategy is to reduce the dependence of the economy on oil through developing new sources of national income to augment and eventually replace oil revenues.

Since the State is the authority which receives and disburses oil revenues, all the major economic policies and variables - development strategy, public and private consumption, public and private investment, structural change, rate of inflation, and so on - have depended on the size and composition of oil revenue disbursements.

Therefore, in order to achieve the objectives outlined in the development strategy and to promote mobilisation and allocation of resources, the government has embarked upon a series of Five-Year Plans, starting with the First FYP in 1976. These plans have contained short- to medium-term objectives, to be achieved through investment programming and appropriate monetary, fiscal and economic policies. The Plan is compulsory for government units in terms of resource mobilisation and investment allocations but, for the private sector, it carries indicative figures of possible investment and consumption patterns.

We shall, therefore, now attempt to identify the role of oil revenues in achieving the government's objectives of growth and structural transformation of the economy.

3.2 Pragmatic orthodoxy in macro-economic management

The availability of oil resources and prudent fiscal management enabled Oman to keep public deficits, as compared to most other developing countries, within the limits the economy could absorb; as a result, it was better able to restrain inflation and manage both internal and external debt. Low inflation and manageable debt has in turn facilitated exchange rate stability. When the macroeconomy did go awry, as a result, for example, of the collapse of oil prices in 1986, the government quickly implemented orthodox solutions, reducing the fiscal deficit and devaluing the currency. Macro-economic stability has been a potent encouragement for growth, investment and capacity building - human and physical. Here we consider briefly the role of oil in enabling Oman to manage successfully four macro-economic fundamentals: budget deficits, inflation, external debt, and exchange rate.

3.2.1 Keeping budget deficits manageable

Oman's budget deficits since 1976 have not been dramatically better than other developing countries, but the distinctive factor has always been that they were within the limits that could be financed without macro-economic instability. Oil revenues have played a very significant role in enabling the government to keep budget deficits low while embarking upon a very ambitious programme of development and transformation. As **Table 3.1** below illustrates, oil revenues have on average provided more than 80 per cent of total revenues, since development planning started in 1976 with the launch of the First FYP.

Table 3.1

Contribution of Oil Revenues to Total Government Revenues Under Four Five-Year Plans (1976-95)

Details	1976-80 Actual (Million RO)	1981-85 Actual (Million RO)	1986-90 Actual (Million RO)	1991-95 Planned (Million RO)
Oil Revenues	3,125	6,649	6,016	8,571
Other Revenues	265	876	1,487	1,570
Total revenues	3,390	7,525	7,503	10,141
Oil Revenues as % of Total Revenues	92.2	88.4	80.2	84.5

Source: Oman, *Five-Year Plans*.

As Chart 3.1 shows, the movement of total government revenues has mirrored the fluctuations in oil revenues arising out of oil price volatility.

Chart 3.1
Index of Government Revenues and Oil Revenues (1985-91)

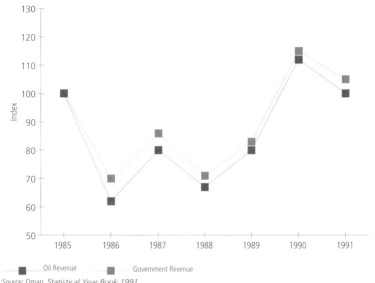

Oil Revenue   Government Revenue
Source: Oman, *Statistical Year Book 1991*.

Due to prudent management, the average annual public deficit as a percentage of GDP over the period 1976-92, and despite the collapse of oil prices in 1986 and the continuous decline since then, has been in the range of 2.6 per cent (**Chapter Annex Table 3.A.1**). Comparing Oman's deficit for the period 1980-88 – the period for which data is available – with other developing economies, Oman's average public deficit for that period was about 3 per cent of GDP, while for 40 developing economies it was about 6.39 per cent of GDP, and 2.82 per cent for OECD economies[7] (**Table 3.2**).

Unlike other economies that have resorted to excessive monetary financing of deficits, heavy government domestic borrowing, and large external financing, which have led in most cases to severe economic crisis, Oman was able to finance its deficits successfully for the following reasons:

a Firstly, as mentioned in Chapter Two, the SGRF and the Contingency Fund – established to act as stabilisers of oil revenues accruing to the treasury – were able to fund from their income a large part of the deficit. In 1986, when the deficit reached about 24 per cent of GDP, the SGRF funded almost 70 per cent of that deficit.

Table 3.2

Consolidated Public Sector Deficits: Oman vs. Selected Economies (1980-88)

Economy/Region	Average Public Deficit, Percentage of GDP, 1980-88
Oman*	3.0
Average: 40 Developing Economies	6.39
Average: OECD Economies	2.82
Other Economies:	
South Korea	1.89
Malaysia	10.8
Thailand	5.8
Philippines	4.3

Source: World Bank, *The East Asian Miracle* (1993), p.109. *For Oman: Chapter Annex Table 3.A.1.

b Secondly, because of the low external debt ratios, Oman was able to access external finance whenever the government thought it prudent to borrow internationally.

3.2.2 Maintaining moderate to low inflation

Unlike many developing economies, Oman kept inflation from spinning out of control. International experience suggests that inflation can be maintained below 20 per cent[8] - a level not breached by Oman since 1971 - for long periods without generating macro-economic instability. Low inflation is a corollary to fiscal prudence. Oman never had to rely on inflation tax because the deficits were within financeable limits.

As **Chart 3.2** below shows, although Oman had a high average annual inflation rate over the period 1965-80, perhaps due to the emergence of the economy in 1970 from a stagnant 'traditional' stage to a 'transitional' forward-looking one, the annual average inflation rate for the period 1980-90 and despite the devaluation of the Omani Rial in 1986, was only 1.12 per cent - the lowest in the world (**Chapter Annex Table 3.A.2**).

The reasons for this very low inflation rate can be summarised as follows:

1 Firstly, oil revenues enabled Oman to have a very liberal import policy, with a minimum level of customs duty - not exceeding 5 per cent for most of the items - with food items and building materials being exempt.

Chart 3.2
Average Annual Inflation Rates: Oman vs. Selected Economies (1965-90)

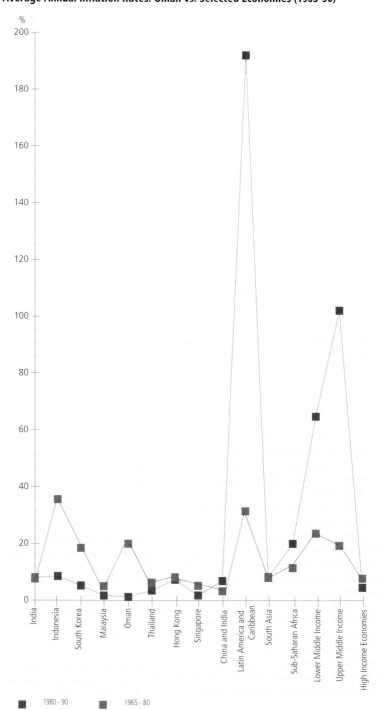

Source : World Bank, *World Development Indicators*, (1992); Oman, Ministry of Development data (1980-90).

Therefore, shortages in domestic production of tradeables were compensated for through imports.

2 Secondly, protection from imports for infant industries was very selective and took the form of increased custom duty - about 25 per cent of the value of the imported goods - instead of import bans, which were the norm in a number of developing countries.

3 Thirdly, while the government adopted development planning as a means of transforming the society and had to interfere in the market mechanism to the extent necessary, the government relied almost exclusively on the markets in trade and production by adopting a 'market-friendly' strategy. This was very clearly emphasised in the development strategy referred to earlier.

4 Fourthly, foreign exchange earnings brought in by oil exports enabled Oman to adopt a liberal exchange system and a stable currency.

3.2.3 Keeping external debt under control

Oil revenues and a conservative foreign borrowing policy have enabled Oman to rely on its internal resources to fund its development strategy while maintaining a comfortable level of external debt. As **Chapter Annex Table 3.A.1** shows, both the debt to GDP ratio and the debt service ratios were fairly low throughout the period 1976-92, with the exception of the period 1986-89 which, as mentioned already, witnessed a drastic fall in oil revenues. As a result, Oman has been able to achieve its objectives of growth and diversification through strict adherence to its Five-Year Plans, without having to resort to externally imposed structural adjustment programmes - with their well-known short-term negative consequences on growth and development - despite the fact that its export price index dropped from 200 in 1982 to about 78 in 1986.[9] However, in the few years when external debt increased, immediate measures were taken to bring it down, and in order to avoid excessive accumulation of external debt throughout the period of the Fourth FYP (1991-95) the Royal Decree No.1/91 (**Appendix VI**) ratifying the plan, stipulated that external public debt should remain at the same level as at the end of the Third FYP. Additional net external borrowing could not be resorted to without the Cabinet's decision.

In view of fairly low indebtedness (**Table 3.3**) as compared to other developing countries, Oman has always enjoyed a high international credit worthiness.

Table 3.3

International Indebtedness: Oman vs. Selected Economies (1992)

Economy/Region	NPV of Total External Debt as % of:		Total Debt Service as:
	Export 1992	GNP 1992	% of Exports 1992
Oman	47.4	27.0	9.0
Malaysia	41.5	35.2	6.6
South Korea	45.8	14.2	7.4
Morocco	222.2	71.2	23.6
Venezuela	214.8	61.1	19.5
Middle-Income Economies	148.2a	34.2a	18.4a
Upper/Middle-Income Economies	143.0a	30.5a	18.9a

Key: NPV = Net Present Value.   Source: World Bank, *World Development Report* (1994).
      a = Average for the region.

3.2.4 Keeping the exchange rate in line

As Todaro[10] states, unpredictable price fluctuations can wreak havoc with both short- and long-range development plans; the government, therefore, believing in the advantages of a stable currency for growth and development, has pegged the Omani Rial to the US dollar since the early 1970s at a rate of US$2.80 equal to one Rial. Needless to say, it was the oil revenues that provided the under-pinning for such a policy.

Reflecting the advantages of stable currency, the Omani Rial stayed fixed to the US dollar until 1986, when, in response to the sharp fall in oil prices, the government devalued the currency by about 10 per cent, thereby changing its dollar value to US$2.60, where it has remained ever since.

3.3   Growth and diversification

Since the objective of planning has been to achieve growth and diversification through the development of oil resources, Oman has been successful in maintaining a high and sustained economic growth. From 1965 to 1980 Oman grew faster than almost all other countries of the world, with the exception of Botswana (**Chart 3.3**) while during the period 1980-90 Oman even overtook Botswana by achieving the highest growth rate (**Chart 3.4**). In this section, we will review the role of oil in propelling this growth, which in turn facilitated high rates of investments, leading to the structural transformation of the economy.

3.3.1 Growth

As Todaro states,[11] in strictly economic terms, 'development' has traditionally meant the capacity of a national economy, whose initial economic condition has been more or less static for a long time, to *generate* and *sustain* an annual increase in its gross national product at rates of not less than 5 per cent.

Similarly, both Lewis,[12] in his 1954 article, and Rostow in various writings on the take-off into self-sustained growth, argued that economic growth, measured by rising per capita income, is the focal defining characteristic of economic development. On the other hand, despite the controversy surrounding the growth theory of development and the calls that were heard in the early 1970s in both the developing and the developed world for the 'dethronement' of GNP as the major objective of economic activity, there is an emerging consensus that economic growth is necessary to achieve development, *albeit* with the qualification that growth on its own does not constitute development. Therefore, in line with its development strategy, Oman put all its efforts into maximising growth, whilst not neglecting the real objective of development, as we shall see later. As a result its nominal GNP[13] grew from a low of RO 111 million in 1972, to RO 3,970 million in 1992, while in constant 1987 Rials, it grew from RO 792 million in 1972 to RO 3,672 million in 1992, thereby achieving an annual average growth rate of about 8 per cent, one of the highest in the world.

At the same time, Oman's GNP per capita grew at more than 6 per cent per annum over the period 1965-90, out-performing every other country in the world (**Chart 3.5** below and **Chapter Annex Table 3.A.3**). In analysing the factors influencing this remarkable achievement, one finds that, in addition to sound macro-economic fundamentals - referred to earlier - oil has undoubtedly played a significant role through:

a Contributing more than 80 per cent of total government revenues (see Chapter Two), which enabled the government to pursue its twin objectives of economic diversification and social change. The growth of non-oil GDP was almost totally influenced by government expenditure (**Chart 3.6** and **Chapter Annex Table 3.A.4**), while the government revenues in turn mirrored the movement of oil GDP (**Chart 3.7** and **Chapter Annex Table 3.A.5**).

b Providing almost 95 per cent of foreign exchange, thereby releasing the resources for importing basic commodities and machinery required for the development process.

Chart 3.3

GDP Average Annual Growth Rates: Oman vs. Selected Countries (1965-80)

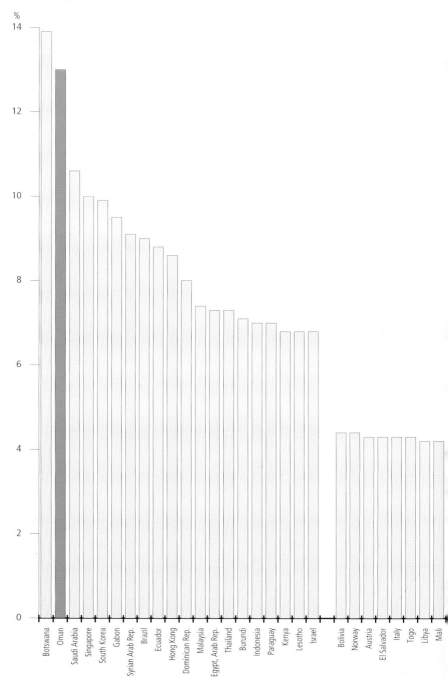

Source : World Bank, *World Development Indicators* (1992).

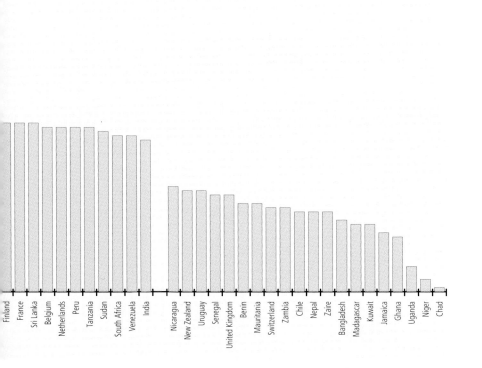

Finland
France
Sri Lanka
Belgium
Netherlands
Peru
Tanzania
Sudan
South Africa
Venezuela
India
Nicaragua
New Zealand
Uruguay
Senegal
United Kingdom
Benin
Mauritania
Switzerland
Zambia
Chile
Nepal
Zaire
Bangladesh
Madagascar
Kuwait
Jamaica
Ghana
Uganda
Niger
Chad

Chart 3.4

GDP Average Annual Growth Rates: Oman vs. Selected Countries (1980-90)

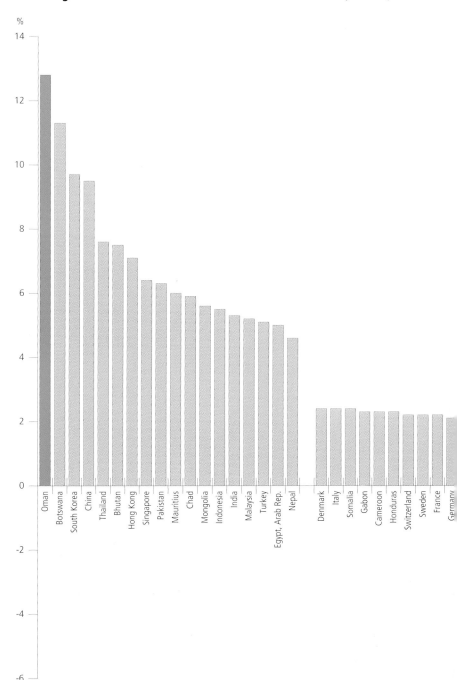

Source : World Bank, *World Development Indicators* (1992).

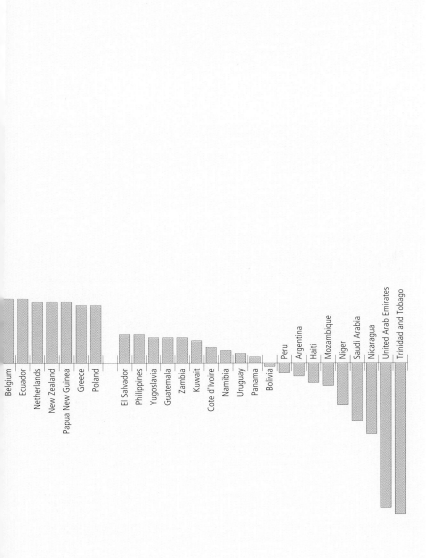

Chart 3.5
Average Annual Growth Rates of GNP per Capita: Oman vs. Selected Economies (1965-90)

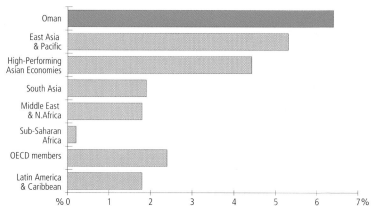

Source : World Bank, *World Development Indicators* (1992).

c Inducing high rates of growth of aggregate income and propelling the rest of the economy along with its growth. The higher rate of domestic savings and investments induced by growth in oil GDP contributed to the diversification process.

3.3.2 Diversification

The diversification of sources of income in the country and the structural transformation of the economy have always been regarded as the principal objectives of Oman's long-term development strategy. However, despite the positive changes that have taken place in the structure of production over the last two decades, it is important to note that achieving sustainable development through a diversified economy normally takes a long time. As per Rostow's 'Stages' theory, the pre-take-off phase in which the preconditions for growth are established could take a hundred years or more.[14]

On the other hand, despite the lack of consensus among development economists about the most appropriate approaches to economic development, one of the most significant and relevant lessons to be learnt from the experience

Chart 3.6

Annual Growth Rates of Total Government Expenditure vs. Annual Growth of non-Oil GDP (1978-93)

Annual % Growth of non-Oil GDP

Annual % Growth of Total Government Expenditure

Source : Oman, *Statistical Year Books.*

Chart 3.7
Government Oil Revenue vs. Oil GDP (1971-93)

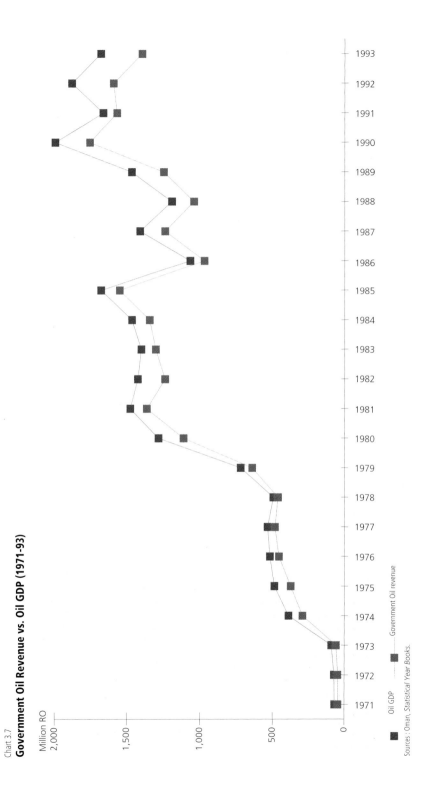

Million RO

2,000

1,500

1,000

500

0

1971
1972
1973
1974
1975
1976
1977
1978
1979
1980
1981
1982
1983
1984
1985
1986
1987
1988
1989
1990
1991
1992
1993

Government Oil revenue

Oil GDP

Sources : Oman, *Statistical Year Books*.

of the last fifty years is the critical importance of concomitant and complementary technological, social, and institutional changes, which must take place if long-term economic growth is to be realised. At the same time, there is no doubt that promoting efficient production and distribution through a proper functioning price system is an integral part of any successful development process.

In Kuznets'[15] analysis, two of the main characteristic features manifested in the growth are: high rates of structural transformation of the economy; and high rates of social and ideological transformation.

As **Chart 3.8** below and **Chapter Annex Table 3.A.6** illustrate, the structure of production has undergone major shifts in the last two decades. Oil and gas, representing primary output in 1970, and accounting for almost 70 per cent of GDP at factor cost, have been declining gradually and stood at about 49 per cent in 1990 and further declined to 38.1 per cent in 1993 (**Chapter Annex Table 3.A.7**). In line with Chenery's[16] empirical findings, as per capita income rose, there was a shift from oil production – being the primary output in the case of Oman as against agriculture for most of the developing countries – to industrial production. The early phase of development was in fact

Chart 3.8
Sectoral Distribution of GDP for Main Sectors (1970-90)

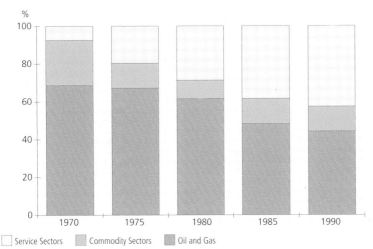

Source: Oman, *Fourth FYP* (1991), p.12.

characterised by dependence (although diminishing) on oil production as a source of income and growth, while the subsequent phase saw a gradual growth of industrial and services output. In fact, in the non-oil commodity producing sector, manufacturing - the most strongly growing of all the components of GDP over a decade and a half - rose from only 0.5 per cent of GDP in 1976 to over 5 per cent in 1993. Agriculture also increased its share, from 2.1 per cent of GDP in 1976 to 3.3 per cent in 1993.

Mirroring the rise in public recurrent spending, public and government services rose from 8 per cent of GDP in 1976 to 11 per cent in 1981, 18 per cent in 1986 and 19 per cent in 1993. However, while the growth of manufacturing and agriculture has been encouraging, their role remains quite minor compared to the share of government services in GDP. If domestically produced non-oil goods and services are to replace oil exports over the remaining life of oil reserves (about 18 years as at 1 January 1994) then manufacturing, agriculture, fishing and tourism must expand considerably in the future.

3.4 Savings and investment

Physical investment includes all of the economy's output that is not either directly consumed or used in the production of other goods. Machines, buildings and infrastructure are physical capital, but elements of working capital, such as inventories, are also important.

A key requirement for any take-off, as articulated by the Lewis model,[17] Rostow's 'Stages of Growth' and the paradigm of expanding capitalist nucleus, is the mobilisation of domestic and foreign savings to spur investment and to accelerate growth.

'The central problem in the theory of economic development is to understand the process by which a community which was previously saving and investing 4 or 5 per cent of the national income, or less, converts itself into an economy where voluntary saving is running at about 12 or 15 per cent of national income or more. This is the central problem because the central fact of economic development is rapid capital accumulation including knowledge and skills with capital (Lewis in Agarwala and Singh)'.[18]

Emphasising the shortage of resources for capital formation, rather than inadequate incentives, Kaldor has stated:

'The importance of public revenue from the point of view of accelerated economic development could hardly be exaggerated. Irrespective of the prevailing ideology or the political color of particular governments, the economic and cultural development of a country requires the efficient and steadily expanding provision of a whole host of non-revenue-yielding services - education, health, communication systems, and so on, commonly known as "infrastructure" - which require to be financed out of government revenue. Besides meeting these needs, taxes or other compulsory levies provide the most appropriate instrument for increasing savings for capital formation out of domestic resources. By reducing the volume of spending by consumers, they make it possible for the resources of the country to be devoted to building up capital assets.'[19]

The statement by Kaldor not only emphasises the shortage of resources for capital formation, but also articulates very strongly the role of government in the process of capital formation.

Realising the importance of rapid capital accumulation in achieving its objective of structural transformation and growth, the government directly and indirectly influenced the level of savings in the economy in order to fund the enormous investments required to meet these objectives. As a result, the share of public investment averaged annually about 19 per cent of GDP between 1976-85, while that of the private sector was 8 per cent; the combined investment by the two sectors averaged about 27 per cent of GDP between 1976-85 (**Chapter Annex Table 3.A.8**).

With the decline of oil prices, the average investment declined to about 18 per cent during 1986-92.

It is worth noting that whilst private investment has declined in line with public investment, its relative share has been rising steadily, reaching about 37 per cent during the same period, compared to its share of only about 18 per cent in 1976. This trend reflects a natural development of the government's policy of encouraging the private sector to take an increasingly active role in the development process (**Chart 3.9**).

On the other hand, although these rates of investment appear high by international standards and are higher than the rates required for the take-off stage, in Rostovian terms they need to be increased further, because oil is a depleting asset, and a substantial portion of the oil proceeds need to be saved in assets that would provide equivalent income when oil finally runs out.

Associated with the question of investment, is the amount of savings that would fund the investment required for the socio-economic transformation.

Chart 3.9
Total Fixed Capital Formation (1989-92)

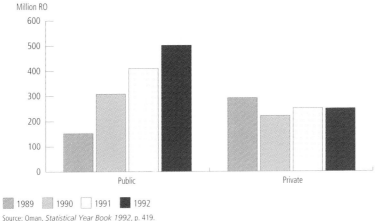

Source: Oman, *Statistical Year Book 1992*, p. 419.

As **Chart 3.10** denotes, savings were very high in the early days of the oil boom, averaging 46.7 per cent of GDP between 1976 and 1981. With the start of the decline in oil prices in 1981, the average declined to 41.8 per cent between 1982-85 and dropped to 31.3 per cent between 1986-91. On the other hand, although national savings (**Chapter Annex Table 3.A.9**) are much lower than domestic savings, reflecting Oman's heavy reliance on foreign contractors and expatriate labour, national savings were quite adequate to fund public and private sector investments – a fact reflected in Oman's virtual zero external debt – since foreign reserves of the SGRF, excluding the Central Bank's monetary reserves, exceeded external debt by the end of 1992.

3.5 Balance of payments

The structure of Oman's balance of payments reflects the characteristics of an economy dependent on oil and oil exports. Crude oil exports for the period 1976-90 accounted, on average, for about 95 per cent of the country's total exports, whilst for the period 1991-93, they accounted for about 87 per cent of total export earnings (**Chapter Annex Table 3.A.10**).

Oman has continuously experienced a large positive trade balance which has enabled it to maintain a stable currency, no restrictions on foreign currency transfers and a liberal import policy.

Chart 3.10
Gross Domestic Savings as a Percentage of GDP (1976-91)

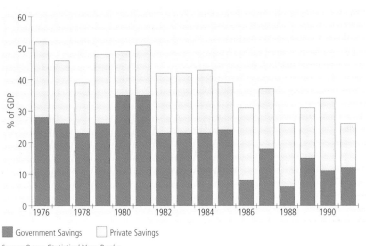

Government Savings   Private Savings

Source: Oman, *Statistical Year Books*.

Due to the dominance of oil exports, the trade balance is typically large during periods of high oil prices such as 1980, 1981, and 1990 and small during periods of low oil prices, such as 1986 and 1988 (**Chart 3.11**).

3.6 Conclusion

We have demonstrated in this chapter that the government, through adoption of a long-term development strategy, which is being implemented through a series of Five-Year Development Plans, has been successful in achieving, over the last two decades, one of the highest rates of growth of aggregate and per capita income. We have also shown that while pragmatic orthodoxy in micro-management undoubtedly contributed to the successful outcome, it was the leading role played by oil resources in inducing higher rates of domestic saving and investment – providing adequate foreign exchange to remove supply shortages and propelling the rest of the economy with its growth – that has been instrumental in achieving diversification of the economy.

Chart 3.11
Recorded Imports, Exports and Trade Balance (1981-92)

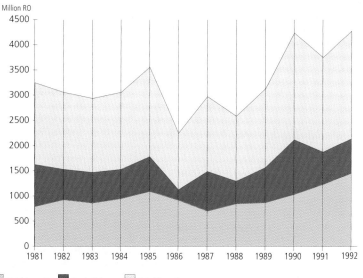

Total Imports ░ Trade Balance ▓ Total Exports ░
Source : Oman, *Statistical Year Book 1992*, p.281.

1	Thirlwall (1990), pp.179-80.	10	Todaro (1992), p.448.
2	Todaro (1992), p.506.	11	Ibid., p.86.
3	Thirlwall (1990), p.60.	12	Hunt (1989), p.62.
4	Oman, *First FYP* (1976), pp.13-14.	13	World Bank, *World Tables* (1994),
5	Hunt (1989), p.98.		p.508.
6	Oman, *Second FYP* (1981), p.58.	14	Hunt (1989), p.99.
7	World Bank, *The East Asian Miracle*	15	Todaro (1992), p.121.
	(1993), p.109.	16	Todaro (1992), pp.74-5
8	Ibid., p.110.	17	Hunt (1989), pp.62-3.
9	World Bank, *World Tables* (1994),	18	Ibid., p.89.
	pp. 510-11.	19	Meier (1989), p.179.

Chapter Annex Table 3.A.1

Major Economic Indicators (1976-92)

Year	R.GDP Growth Rate (%) (1978=100%)	Inflation Rate: GDP Deflator (1978=100%)	Debt/GDP (%)	Debt/ Service Ratio (%)	Trade Balance/ GDP (%)	Private Invest- ment/GDP (%)	Public Invest- ment/GDP (%)	Budget Deficit/ GDP (%)	MI/GDP (%)
1976	NA	NA	4.8	3.2	18.9	6.5	29.4	7.5	11.6
1977	NA	NA	7.8	3.4	16.7	7.5	23.1	-1.5	12.0
1978	0.0	0.0	6.8	6.8	12.0	9.2	19.7	-6.1	12.3
1979	1.2	34.6	4.0	5.9	22.9	9.3	16.7	3.2	9.8
1980	6.0	50.9	2.5	5.6	29.9	7.7	14.8	12.8	7.7
1981	17.0	3.1	4.1	4.6	31.7	7.8	15.6	12.2	8.8
1982	11.5	-5.9	5.5	7.3	20.5	8.6	18.4	-1.3	9.3
1983	16.0	-9.6	11.2	6.7	20.6	7.6	19.3	-2.8	9.9
1984	16.7	-4.7	15.0	6.9	16.9	8.6	21.4	-7.1	9.6
1985	13.8	-0.4	15.3	7.0	16.1	7.3	20.3	-3.9	9.5
1986	3.4	-21.6	26.6	20.8	4.0	8.8	23.3	-23.5	11.1
1987	-3.5	11.1	23.1	20.8	23.5	5.5	13.3	-2.6	11.1
1988	5.7	-7.8	26.2	11.8	13.2	12.1	5.4	-10.7	10.7
1989	3.1	7.1	24.8	13.6	20.2	9.0	4.7	-4.7	10.7
1990	7.5	16.6	16.5	11.0	25.7	5.5	7.6	4.6	9.6
1991	9.2	-11.4	16.9	10.7	15.2	6.4	10.5	-0.2	10.3
1992	6.8	5.6	20.4	10.7	14.4	5.6	11.4	-6.3	9.6

Source: Oman, Ministry of Development data.

Chapter Annex Table 3.A.2

Average Annual Inflation Rates: Oman vs. Selected Economies (1965-90)

Economies	Inflation: Average Annual Rate (%) 1965-80	Inflation: Average Annual Rate (%) 1980-90
India	7.5	7.9
Indonesia	35.5	8.4
South Korea	18.4	5.1
Malaysia	4.9	1.6
Oman	19.9	1.12
Thailand	6.2	3.4
Hong Kong	8.1	7.2
Singapore	5.1	1.7
China	-0.3	5.8
East Asia & Pacific	9.3	6.0
Latin America & Caribbean	31.4	192.1
Middle East & N. Africa	13.6	7.5
South Asia	8.3	8.0
Sub-Saharan Africa	11.4	20.0
Lower/Middle-Income Economies	23.6	64.8
Other Low-Income Economies	17.3	15.1
Upper/Middle-Income Economies	19.3	102.1
High-Income Economies	7.7	4.5
Low- and Middle-Income Economies	16.7	61.8
Low-Income Economies	8.0	9.6
Middle-Income Economies	21.1	85.6
World	9.2	14.7

Source: World Bank, *World Development Indicators* (1992); Oman, Ministry of Development data (1986-90 only).

Average Annual Growth Rates of GNP per Capita: Oman vs. Selected Countries (1965-90)

Country	GNP per Capita: Average Annual Growth Rate (%) 1965-90	Selected High Performing Asian Economies	GNP per Capita: Average Annual Growth Rate (%) 1965-90
		Indonesia	4.5
Sub-Saharan Africa	0.2		
		Thailand	4.4
Middle East & N. Africa	1.8	Malaysia	4.0
Latin America & Caribbean	1.8	South Korea	7.1
		Singapore	6.5
South Asia	1.9		
		Hong Kong	6.2
OECD Members	2.4		
East Asia & Pacific	5.3		
High-Performing Asian Economies	5.5		
Oman	6.4	Source: World Bank, *World Development Indicators* (1992).	

Chapter Annex Table 3.A.4

Growth of Government Expenditure vs. non-Oil GDP Growth (1976-93)

Year	Total Government Expenditure (Million RO)	Annual Growth (%)	Non-Oil GDP (Million RO)	Annual Growth (%)
1976	553.5		373.8	
1977	534.8	-3.38	422.3	12.97
1978	560.1	4.73	463.5	9.76
1979	650.4	16.12	583.0	25.78
1980	924.7	42.17	800.0	37.22
1981	1174.7	27.04	1044.4	30.55
1982	1369.0	16.54	1221.9	17.00
1983	1500.9	9.63	1388.7	13.65
1984	1728.5	15.16	1631.9	17.51
1985	1909.6	10.48	1801.2	10.37
1986	1879.5	-1.58	1771.5	-1.65
1987	1589.5	-15.43	1641.3	-7.35
1988	1560.7	-1.81	1779.9	8.44
1989	1633.9	4.69	1820.2	2.26
1990	1851.7	13.33	2149.3	18.08
1991	1851.5	-0.01	2312.0	7.57
1992	2209.4	19.33	2594.1	12.2
1993	2190.0	-0.88	2800.5	7.96

Source: Oman, *Statistical Year Books*.

Chapter Annex Table 3.A.5

Growth of Government Oil Revenues vs. Oil GDP Growth (1971-93)

Year	Government Oil Revenues (Million RO)	Annual Growth (%)	Oil GDP (Million RO)	Annual Growth (%)
1971	47.9		73.9	
1972	49.6	3.5	76.4	3.4
1973	61.4	23.8	94.5	23.7
1974	291.5	374.8	389.0	311.6
1975	373.1	28.0	486.8	25.1
1976	454.7	21.9	517.5	6.3
1977	482.2	6.0	532.8	3.0
1978	457.7	-4.1	493.0	-7.5
1979	638.9	39.6	718.9	45.8
1980	1095.5	71.5	1279.5	78.0
1981	1341.3	22.4	1473.8	15.2
1982	1215.7	-9.4	1420.9	-3.6
1983	1277.5	5.1	1396.5	-1.7
1984	1304.6	2.1	1461.4	4.6
1985	1510.0	15.7	1675.1	14.6
1986	928.9	-38.5	1063.1	-36.5
1987	1194.9	28.6	1404.7	32.1
1988	993.6	-16.8	1187.1	-15.5
1989	1197.4	20.5	1462.0	23.2
1990	1701.6	42.1	1990.3	36.1
1991	1515.7	-10.9	1658.4	-16.7
1992	1525.1	0.6	1875.1	13.1
1993	1331.6	-12.7	1673.6	-10.7

Source: Oman, *Statistical Year Books*.

Chapter Annex Table 3.A.6

Growth of GDP by Major Sectors (1970-90)
(in Million RO)

Details	1970	1975	End of First Five-Year Plan (1980)	End of Second Five-Year Plan (1985)	End of Third Five-Year Plan (1990)
(1) Oil Sectors					
Crude Oil	72	487	1,267	1,639	1,942.7
Natural Gas	-	-	12	36	47.6
Total Oil Sectors	72	487	1,279	1,675	1,990.3
Non-Oil Sectors					
(a) Commodity Sectors					
Mining	-	-	1	9	11.9
Agriculture	12	14	37	68	84.7
Fisheries	4	6	15	26	49.1
Industry	-	2	16	82	155.9
Electricity & Water	-	2	16	37	46.8
Building & Construction	9	71	118	242	123.3
Total (a)	25	95	203	464	471.7
(b) Service Sectors					
Government Services	2	53	195	478	658.6
Other Services	6	90	402	860	1,011.9
Total (b)	8	143	597	1,338	1,670.5
(2) Total non-Oil Sectors (a + b)	33	238	800	1,802	2,142.2
Minus					
(c) Imputed Banking Services	(1)	(3)	(25)	(64)	(121.8)
Plus					
(d) Customs Duties			9	41	32.9
(3) Total (c + d)	(1)	(3)	(16)	(23)	(88.9)
(4) GDP at Producers' Current Prices (1 + 2 + 3)	104	722	2,063	3,454	4,043.6

Source: Oman, *Statistical Year Books*.

GDP by Kind of Economic Activity (1976-93) (%)

Economic Activity	First FYP					Second FYP	
	1976	1977	1978	1979	1980	1981	1982
A Industries							
1. Agriculture, Hunting, Forestry & Fishing	**2.1**	**2.5**	**3.2**	**3.1**	**2.5**	**2.5**	**2.5**
a) Agriculture & Livestock	1.4	1.8	2.4	2.4	1.8	1.6	1.7
b) Fishing	0.7	0.7	0.8	0.7	0.7	0.9	0.8
2. Mining & Quarries	**58.5**	**56.3**	**52.1**	**55.8**	**62.1**	**59.3**	**54.5**
a) Crude Petroleum	58.5	56.3	51.9	55.3	61.4	58.5	53.6
b) Natural Gas	0.0	0.0	0.2	0.5	0.6	0.7	0.7
c) Non-Ferrous Ores	0.0	0.0	0.0	0.0	0.0	0.0	0.0
d) Stone Quarrying, Clay & Sand Pits	0.0	0.0	0.1	0.1	0.0	0.1	0.1
3. Manufacturing	**0.5**	**0.7**	**0.9**	**0.9**	**0.8**	**1.1**	**1.5**
a) Oil Refinery	0.0	0.0	0.0	0.0	0.0	0.0	0.0
b) Other	0.5	0.7	0.9	0.9	0.8	1.1	1.5
4. Electric Light & Power	**0.7**	**1.0**	**1.1**	**0.9**	**0.8**	**0.8**	**0.8**
a) Electric Light & Power	0.5	0.7	0.9	0.7	0.6	0.6	0.6
b) Water Works & Supply	0.2	0.3	0.2	0.2	0.2	0.2	0.2
5. Construction	**10.0**	**8.2**	**7.5**	**6.7**	**5.7**	**5.8**	**6.5**
6 Trade – Wholesale & Retail, Restaurants & Hotels	**8.7**	**9.9**	**11.0**	**10.6**	**9.1**	**10.1**	**11.5**
a) Wholesale & Retail Trade	8.6	9.8	10.8	10.5	8.9	9.7	11.0
b) Restaurants, Cafes & Other Eating and Drinking Places	0.0	0.1	0.1	0.2	0.1	0.1	0.2
c) Hotels, Rooming Houses & Other Lodgings	0.0	0.0	0.0	0.0	0.1	0.2	0.2
7. Transport, Storage & Communications	**1.5**	**1.9**	**2.2**	**2.0**	**1.9**	**2.2**	**2.5**
a) Passenger Land Transport	0.6	0.8	0.9	0.7	0.5	0.5	0.6
b) Freight Transport by Road	0.9	1.1	1.3	1.2	1.0	1.2	1.3
c) Communications	0.0	0.0	0.0	0.0	0.3	0.5	0.6
8. Financial, Insurance, Real Estate and Business Services	**10.4**	**10.2**	**10.6**	**9.5**	**7.9**	**8.3**	**8.8**
a) Financial Institutions (Banking)	1.3	1.5	1.5	1.5	1.5	1.8	2.0
b) Insurance	0.0	0.0	0.0	0.2	0.2	0.2	0.4
c) Real Estate	7.5	7.3	7.7	6.6	5.2	5.3	5.3
d) Legal, Accounting, Auditing, Book-Keeping	0.0	0.1	0.1	0.1	0.0	0.0	0.0
e) Engineering, Architecture & Technical Services	1.6	1.4	1.3	1.2	1.0	1.0	1.2

continued

	Second FYP			Third FYP					Fourth FYP		
	1983	1984	1985	1986	1987	1988	1989	1990	1991	1992	1993
	2.9	2.9	2.7	3.4	3.5	4.2	3.6	3.3	3.7	3.3	3.3
	2.0	1.9	2.0	2.4	2.3	2.7	2.6	2.1	2.4	2.1	2.2
	0.9	1.0	0.8	1.0	1.2	1.6	1.0	1.2	1.3	1.2	1.1
	51.2	48.2	48.8	38.3	47.0	41.1	45.8	49.4	42.6	42.7	38.1
	50.0	46.9	47.5	36.6	45.3	39.1	43.9	48.0	41.1	41.2	36.5
	0.9	1.1	1.0	1.4	1.4	1.5	1.4	1.2	1.3	1.2	1.4
	0.0	0.1	0.1	0.1	0.2	0.4	0.3	0.2	0.1	0.1	0.1
	0.2	0.2	0.2	0.2	0.1	0.1	0.2	0.1	0.1	0.1	0.2
	1.8	2.4	2.4	3.7	3.7	4.2	4.2	3.8	4.3	4.3	5.2
	0.1	0.4	0.3	0.3	0.3	0.4	0.4	0.4	0.4	0.5	0.9
	1.7	2.0	2.1	3.4	3.4	3.8	3.8	3.4	3.9	3.8	4.3
	0.9	1.1	1.1	1.4	1.4	1.6	1.5	1.5	1.6	1.5	1.3
	0.6	0.8	0.8	1.1	0.9	1.0	0.9	0.9	0.9	0.8	0.7
	0.3	0.3	0.3	0.3	0.5	0.6	0.6	0.6	0.7	0.7	0.6
	6.8	7.4	7.0	7.9	4.6	4.3	3.3	3.0	3.9	4.0	4.1
	11.5	12.1	12.4	13.7	10.9	13.3	12.2	11.6	13.8	13.9	15.0
	11.1	11.6	11.9	13.1	10.3	12.6	11.5	11.0	13.1	13.2	14.3
	0.2	0.2	0.2	0.3	0.3	0.4	0.3	0.3	0.4	0.4	0.4
	0.3	0.2	0.2	0.3	0.2	0.3	0.3	0.3	0.3	0.3	0.3
	2.7	2.8	2.9	3.7	3.2	3.7	3.5	3.2	3.7	3.6	4.0
	0.6	0.6	0.6	0.8	0.8	0.9	0.8	0.7	0.8	0.8	0.8
	1.3	1.3	1.4	1.4	1.6	1.3	1.6	1.4	1.3	1.6	1.8
	0.7	0.8	0.9	1.2	1.1	1.3	1.3	1.2	1.4	1.3	1.4
	9.1	9.1	8.6	10.0	8.9	9.2	9.0	8.8	8.8	8.4	9.3
	2.1	2.2	2.1	2.8	2.5	2.6	2.7	3.0	2.5	2.4	2.6
	0.3	0.4	0.5	0.5	0.6	0.4	0.4	0.4	0.4	0.4	0.5
	5.6	5.1	4.6	5.1	4.9	5.3	5.1	4.7	5.0	4.8	5.2
	0.1	0.1	0.1	0.1	0.1	0.1	0.1	0.1	0.1	0.1	0.1
	1.2	1.3	1.2	1.4	0.8	0.7	0.7	0.6	0.8	0.8	0.8

Chapter Annex Table 3.A.7 continued

Economic Activity	First FYP					Second FYP	
	1976	1977	1978	1979	1980	1981	1982
9. Community & Personal Services	**0.5**	**0.6**	**0.8**	**0.7**	**0.6**	**0.7**	**0.8**
a) Education Services	0.0	0.0	0.1	0.1	0.1	0.1	0.1
b) Medical, Dental & Others	0.0	0.0	0.0	0.0	0.0	0.0	0.0
c) Motion Picture Distribution & Projection	0.0	0.0	0.0	0.0	0.0	0.0	0.0
d) Repair of Motor Vehicles and Motor Cycles	0.2	0.3	0.3	0.3	0.2	0.2	0.3
e) Launderers & Laundry Service, Cleaning & Dyeing	0.0	0.0	0.0	0.0	0.0	0.0	0.0
f) Domestic Services	0.3	0.3	0.3	0.3	0.3	0.3	0.3
g) Barber & Beauty Shops	0.0	0.0	0.0	0.0	0.0	0.0	0.0
10. Inputed Bank Service Charges	**-1.2**	**-1.4**	**-1.5**	**-1.5**	**-1.2**	**-1.6**	**-1.7**
TOTAL INDUSTRIES (1 TO 10)	**91.7**	**90.0**	**88.0**	**88.8**	**90.2**	**89.1**	**87.8**
B. Producers of Govt Services	**7.8**	**9.6**	**11.5**	**10.7**	**9.4**	**10.5**	**11.7**
a) Agriculture & Fishing	6.7	8.0	0.3	0.2	0.2	0.2	0.3
b) Transport & Communications	0.0	0.0	0.0	0.3	0.3	0.3	0.3
c) Public Administration & Defence	0.0	0.0	9.4	8.5	7.4	8.3	9.0
d) Education	0.7	1.0	1.2	1.1	1.1	1.2	1.5
e) Health	0.4	0.5	0.6	0.6	0.5	0.5	0.6
C. Grand Total: GDP at Producer's Values (A + B)	**99.5**	**99.5**	**99.5**	**99.5**	**99.6**	**99.5**	**99.4**
D. Plus Import Duties	**0.5**	**0.5**	**0.5**	**0.5**	**0.4**	**0.5**	**0.6**
E. GDP at Producer's Values (C + D)	**100.0**	**100.0**	**100.0**	**100.0**	**100.0**	**100.0**	**100.0**

Source: Oman, *Statistical Year Books*.

	Second FYP			Third FYP					Fourth FYP		
	1983	1984	1985	1986	1987	1988	1989	1990	1991	1992	1993
0.9	**1.0**	**1.0**	**1.4**	**1.3**	**1.6**	**1.5**	**1.4**	**1.8**	**1.7**	**0.9**
0.1	0.1	0.1	0.2	0.2	0.2	0.2	0.2	0.3	0.3	0.3
0.0	0.0	0.0	0.1	0.1	0.1	0.1	0.1	0.1	0.1	0.2
0.0	0.0	0.0	0.0	0.0	0.0	0.0	0.0	0.0	0.0	0.0
0.3	0.3	0.3	0.4	0.4	0.4	0.4	0.4	0.4	0.4	0.4
0.0	0.0	0.0	0.0	0.0	0.0	0.1	0.1	0.1	0.1	0.1
0.4	0.4	0.4	0.5	0.5	0.7	0.6	0.5	0.8	0.6	0.7
0.1	0.1	0.1	0.1	0.1	0.1	0.1	0.1	0.1	0.1	0.2
-1.8	**-1.9**	**-1.8**	**-2.5**	**-2.3**	**-2.5**	**-2.5**	**-3.0**	**-2.4**	**-2.2**	**-2.2**
86.1	**85.0**	**85.0**	**81.0**	**82.2**	**80.7**	**82.1**	**82.9**	**81.9**	**81.4**	**80.0**
13.1	**13.9**	**13.8**	**17.7**	**16.9**	**18.3**	**17.0**	**16.3**	**17.1**	**17.5**	**19.0**
0.3	0.3	0.2	0.3	0.3	0.3	0.3	0.3	0.3	0.3	0.3
0.4	0.4	0.4	0.4	0.3	0.4	0.3	0.3	0.3	0.3	0.3
10.3	10.9	10.8	13.7	13.0	13.6	12.5	11.6	12.2	12.4	13.3
1.6	1.6	1.7	2.3	2.3	2.6	2.6	2.9	3.1	3.3	3.7
0.7	0.7	0.8	1.0	1.1	1.3	1.3	1.2	1.2	1.2	1.3
99.2	**99.0**	**98.8**	**98.7**	**99.1**	**99.0**	**99.1**	**99.2**	**99.0**	**98.9**	**99.0**
0.8	**1.0**	**1.2**	**1.3**	**0.9**	**1.0**	**0.9**	**0.8**	**1.0**	**1.1**	**1.0**
100.0	**100.0**	**100.0**	**100.0**	**100.0**	**100.0**	**100.0**	**100.0**	**100.0**	**100.0**	**100.0**

Chapter Annex Table 3.A.8

Expenditure on GDP at Purchasers' Value (1976-93)

Year	Consumption			Fixed Capital Formation			Net Export of Goods & Services (%)	GDP at Purchasers' Value (2 + 5 + 8) (%)
	Total (%) (3 + 4)	Private * (%)	Public (%)	Total (%) (6 + 7)	Private (%)	Public (%)		
(1)	(2)	(3)	(4)	(5)	(6)	(7)	(8)	(9)
First FYP								
1976	47.8	20.5	27.3	35.9	6.5	29.4	16.3	100.0
1977	54.4	26.0	28.4	30.6	7.5	23.1	15.0	100.0
1978	61.5	32.8	28.7	28.9	9.2	19.7	9.6	100.0
1979	53.7	26.2	27.5	26.0	9.3	16.7	20.3	100.0
1980	52.1	27.9	24.2	22.6	7.8	14.8	25.3	100.0
Second FYP								
1981	50.1	23.7	26.4	23.4	7.8	15.6	26.5	100.0
1982	57.8	30.4	27.4	27.0	8.6	18.4	15.2	100.0
1983	57.7	29.3	28.5	26.9	7.6	19.3	15.4	100.0
1984	57.3	30.8	26.5	30.0	8.6	21.4	12.7	100.0
1985	59.8	32.6	27.2	27.6	7.3	20.3	12.6	100.0
Third FYP								
1986	69.6	36.4	33.2	32.1	8.8	23.3	-1.7	100.0
1987	61.4	31.0	30.4	18.8	5.5	13.3	19.8	100.0
1988	73.0	32.7	40.3	17.5	12.1	5.4	9.5	100.0
1989	70.0	30.2	39.8	13.8	9.1	4.7	16.2	100.0
1990	64.8	26.7	38.1	13.1	5.5	7.6	22.1	100.0
Fourth FYP								
1991	73.5	37.9	35.6	16.9	6.4	10.5	9.6	100.0
1992	72.6	33.4	39.2	17.2	5.8	11.4	10.2	100.0
1993	76.1	39.4	36.7	18.1	6.9	11.2	5.8	100.0

* Including changes in stocks.

Source: Oman, *Statistical Year Books*.

Chapter Annex Table 3.A.9

Domestic and National Savings (1976-93)
(In Million RO)

Year	GDP at Purchasers' Price	Total Final Consumption	Domestic Savings (2-3)	Net Factor Income (Transfers)	National Savings (4-5)	Domestic Savings as % of GDP	National Savings as % of GDP	GNP (2-5)
(1)	(2)	(3)	(4)	(5)	(6)	(7)	(8)	(9)
1976	884.3	422.5	461.8	-148.0	313.8	52.2	35.5	736.3
1977	946.8	514.7	432.1	-130.0	302.1	45.6	31.9	816.8
1978	946.9	582.6	364.3	-111.0	253.3	38.5	26.8	835.9
1979	1,289.9	692.1	597.8	-137.0	460.8	46.3	35.7	1,152.9
1980	2,063.5	1,076.0	987.5	-212.0	775.5	47.9	37.6	1,851.5
1981	2,490.5	1,247.0	1,243.5	-235.0	1,008.5	49.9	40.5	2,255.5
1982	2,613.6	1,509.9	1,103.7	-238.0	865.7	42.2	33.1	2,375.6
1983	2,739.9	1,582.0	1,157.9	-297.0	860.9	42.3	31.4	2,442.9
1984	3,046.7	1,746.5	1,300.2	-350.0	950.0	42.7	31.2	2,696.7
1985	3,453.8	2,063.7	1,390.1	-399.0	991.1	40.3	28.7	3,054.8
1986	2,800.4	1,949.0	851.4	-336.0	515.4	30.4	18.4	2,464.4
1987	3,002.6	1,843.3	1,159.3	-281.0	878.3	38.6	29.3	2,721.6
1988	2,925.9	2,135.8	790.1	-408.0	382.1	27.0	13.1	2,517.9
1989	3,230.6	2,260.4	970.2	-404.0	566.2	30.0	17.5	2,826.7
1990	4,050.7	2,625.5	1,425.2	-419.0	1,006.2	35.2	24.8	3,631.7
1991	3,917.4	2,880.0	1,037.4	-415.0	622.4	26.5	15.9	3,502.4
1992	4,421.8	3,210.2	1,211.6	-573.0	638.6	27.4	14.4	3,848.8
1993	4,419.7	3,364.8	1,054.9	-592.0	462.9	23.9	10.5	3,827.7

Source: Oman, *Statistical Year Books.*

Chapter Annex Table 3.A.10

Balance of Payments (1976-93)
(In Million RO)

Items	1976	1977	1978	1979	1980	1981	1982	1983
Trade Balance	167	158	114	295	616	789	537	564
Exports & Re-exports	551	559	552	788	1294	1622	1528	1470
Oil Exports	544	546	522	746	1244	1526	1410	1347
Non-Oil Exports	7	13	30	42	50	96	118	123
– Other Exports	1	1	3	5	5	7	8	11
– Re-Exports	6	12	27	37	45	89	110	112
Imports	-384	-401	-438	-493	-678	-833	-991	-906
Recorded	-251	-310	-327	-431	-615	-790	-927	-861
Unrecorded	-133	-91	-111	-62	-63	-43	-64	-45
% of Oil Exports to Total Exports	98.7	97.7	94.6	94.7	96.1	94.1	92.3	91.6
Service Balance (1 + 2)	-170	-154	-134	-169	-323	-364	-378	-440
1. Non Factor Services	-22	-24	-23	-32	-111	-129	-140	-143
Travel	0	0	0	0	-11	-12	-12	-15
Port Dues	0	0	0	0	0	3	4	5
Other Services	-22	-24	-23	-32	-100	-119	-131	-132
Other Private Current Transfers	0	0	0	0	0	-1	-1	-1
2. Factor Payment	-148	-130	-111	-137	-212	-235	-238	-297
Property & Enterprise	-72	-54	-38	-51	-87	-77	-47	-58
– Profit Remittance	-74	-52	-40	-44	-97	-122	-139	-143
– Official Interest	2	-2	2	-7	7	36	82	70
– Commercial Bank Interest	0	0	0	0	3	9	10	15
Net Workers' Remittances	-76	-76	-73	-86	-125	-158	-191	-239
Current Account Balance	-3	4	-20	126	293	425	159	124

Source: Oman, *Statistical Year Book 1985*, p.323; Oman, *Statistical Year Book 1993*, pp.345-46.

1984	1985	1986	1987	1988	1989	1990	1991	1992	1993
514	555	113	707	385	654	1042	594	636	411
1527	1717	1093	1463	1285	1564	2118	1873	2136	2063
1401	1597	981	1339	1130	1396	1942	1629	1786	1621
126	120	112	124	155	168	176	244	350	442
17	23	27	39	63	67	69	79	97	122
109	97	85	85	92	101	107	165	253	320
-1013	-1162	-980	-756	-900	-910	-1076	-1279	-1500	-1652
-949	-1089	-917	-701	-846	-869	-1031	-1228	-1449	-1582
-64	-73	-63	-55	-54	-41	-45	-51	-51	-70
91.7	93	89.8	91.5	87.9	89.3	91.7	87	83.6	78.6
-477	-517	-496	-379	-514	-526	-579	-654	-770	-759
-127	-118	-160	-112	-106	-120	-160	-231	-197	-167
-17	-18	-18	-18	-18	-18	-18	-18	-18	-18
5	5	5	5	5	4	4	5	5	5
-114	-104	-147	-99	-93	-106	-146	-218	-184	-154
-1	-1	0	0	0	0	0	0	0	0
-350	-399	-336	-267	-408	-406	-419	-423	-573	-592
-68	-87	-13	3	-115	-102	-105	-88	-119	-81
-151	-167	-165	-134	-130	-131	-149	-156	-168	-176
61	69	145	129	4	14	30	58	45	89
22	11	7	8	11	15	14	10	4	6
-282	-312	-232	-270	-293	-304	-314	-335	-454	-511
37	38	-383	328	-129	128	463	-60	-134	-348

Chapter Four

Oil and the Human Dimension of Development

In Chapter Three, we referred briefly to the growing concern that emerged during the 1960s Development Decade with regard to the apparent absence of a 'trickle-down' effect from economic growth. A number of developing countries that experienced relatively high rates of per capita income growth during the 1960s and 1970s had shown little or no improvement or even actual decline in employment, equality, and the real income of the bottom 40 per cent of their populations. This concern was voiced, *interalia*, by Dudley Seers in 1972:

> 'The questions to ask about a country's development are therefore: what has been happening to poverty? What has been happening to unemployment? What has been happening to inequality? If all three of these have declined from high levels, then beyond doubt this has been a period of development for the country concerned. If one or two of these problems have been growing worse, especially if all three have, it would be strange to call the result "development", even if per capita income doubled.' [1]

As a result, during the 1970s, economic development came to be redefined in terms of the reduction or elimination of poverty, inequality, and unemployment within the context of a growing economy. 'Redistribution from Growth' became a common slogan. [2]

Although contemporary debate on development theory and policy does not reflect a unanimity of analytical perspective, there is an emerging consensus that the real objective of development is to increase peoples' development choices. Income is one aspect of the choices – and an extremely important one – but it is not the sum-total of human existence. Health, education, a good physical environment and freedom – to name a few other components of well-being – may be just as important.

It is important to point out that growth in income and an expansion of economic opportunities are necessary preconditions for human development. As Seers argued, '. . . for how else could mass welfare continue to rise over time? Although growth is not the end of development, the absence of growth often is.'[3]

Emphasis on shared growth, reducing inequality and human development have been the principal elements of Oman's development strategy:

> 'It is necessary to effect a wider geographical distribution of investments in order that the benefits may be shared by different regions to the greatest possible extent and to narrow the gap in the standards of living in different regions with special emphasis on the least developed regions . . .' (Article 5, Oman's Development Strategy, 1975.)

> 'Care should be taken to develop the local human resources...In this respect, it is necessary to extend and develop educational and training programmes, to improve nutritional and public health conditions . . .'[4] (Article 6, Ibid.)

Despite the lack of a widely accepted Physical Quality of Life Indicator, we shall, by using the indicators of basic need performance suggested by Hicks/Streeten[5] (**Chapter Annex Table 4.A.1**), evaluate briefly the extent to which the benefits of growth and structural transformation have enhanced human development in terms of health, education, equality and employment. These indicators have been selected as an alternative measure of development since they appear to be free of the major problems associated with the use of GNP as a measure of development; they are standardised and accepted indicators and are the stated objectives of the development plans of most developing countries.

In fact, the development diamond (**Chart 4.1**) developed by the World Bank to portray relationships among four socio-economic indicators for a given country and to compare them with the average of the country's income group, clearly demonstrates Oman's remarkable achievements compared to its peers in the health and education sectors.

Chart 4.1
Development Diamond

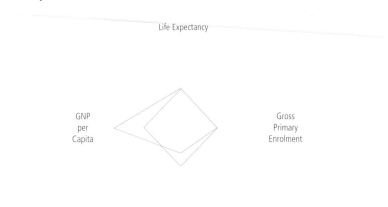

Life Expectancy

GNP per Capita

Gross Primary Enrolment

Access to Safe Drinking Water

*Based on four key socio-economic indicators: GNP per capita, life expectancy,
primary school enrolment and access to safe drinking water.

Source: World Bank, *Social Indicators of Development* (1994).

4.1 Health

A long life may not guarantee that people develop their talents and achieve their goals, but it increases the chances that they will.

As the development diamond indicates, Oman's performance in the health sector has been remarkable, considering the desperate situation prevailing before 1970 (see Chapter One). By analysing the data in Oman's 1990 Statistical Year Book, it can be seen that annual growth rates for the period 1971-90 averaged 16 per cent for hospital beds, 17.6 per cent for doctors, 22.3 per cent for nurses, 22.3 per cent for in-patients and 83.5 per cent for out-patients (**Chapter Annex Table 4.A.2**). Currently, over 90 per cent of the population has ready access to permanent or mobile facilities providing them with both preventive and curative health services.

As can be seen from **Table 4.1** below, immense progress has been made in the output of the health sector, as demonstrated by the increase in life expectancy from 57 years in 1980 to 67.1 years in 1993 (life expectancy was 49 years during 1970-75), while infant mortality rate has dropped from 64 per 1000 births in 1980 to 23 in 1993.

Table 4.1

Estimated National Vital Rates (1980-93)

Selected Years	Birth Rate (a) (c)	Death Rate of Infants (b) (d)	Natural Increase Rate (e)	Life Expectancy at Birth (Years)
1980	50.0	64.0	37.0	57.0
1984	49.0	48.0	38.0	60.8
1985	48.0	45.0	38.0	61.6
1988	46.0	34.0	38.0	65.7
1989	45.4	31.0	38.0	66.3
1990	44.7	29.0	37.0	66.5
1991	43.9	27.0	37.0	66.7
1992	42.2	25.0	37.0	66.9
1993	40.3	23.0	37.0	67.1

(a) Per 1,000 population
(b) Per 1,000 live births
(c) Results obtained by applying age-specific fertility rates found in 1988 Child Health Survey to the age/sex distribution of population.
(d) 55 in 1982 and 45 in 1985 (Child Mortality Survey, 1986); 34 in 1988 (Child Health Survey, 1988); interpolation and extrapolation for other years.
(e) Results obtained by applying western life tables to estimated age/sex distibution of population.

Source: Oman, Ministry of Health, *The Annual Statistical Report 1994*, p.16.

As a testimony to the progress made in health services, Unicef's 1994 report[6] stated that Oman had achieved a 97 per cent rate of immunisation against measles – against a goal of 90 per cent to be achieved by the year 2000. In terms of doctors and nurses, in 1990 Oman had 1,060 persons per doctor and 2,810 persons per nurse, compared with the average of 3,410 persons per doctor and 3,940 persons per nurse for countries ranked in the medium human development category – into which Oman falls.[7] **Chart 4.2** and **Chart 4.3** below indicate respectively Oman's life expectancy at birth and infant mortality rate as compared with high and medium development countries. The emerging picture is highly commendable.

In order to achieve these improvements, the government has been allocating about 10 to 11 per cent of its annual current expenditure to health care. The role of the private sector up to now has been very limited in this sector, because health services are provided almost free to all Omanis (**Chapter Annex Table 4.A.3**).

Chart 4.2

Life Expectancy at Birth: Oman vs. Medium and High Human Development Countries (1960, 1992)

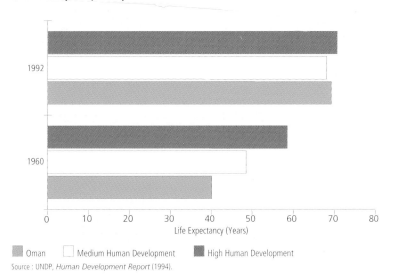

Source : UNDP, *Human Development Report* (1994).

Chart 4.3

Infant Mortality Rates: Oman vs. Medium and High Human Development Countries (1960, 1992)

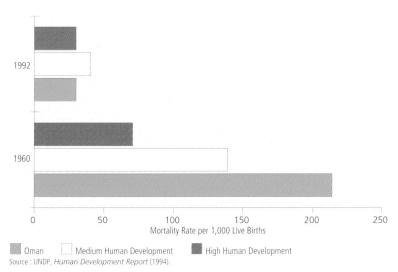

Source : UNDP, *Human Development Report* (1994).

4.2 Education

Most economists would probably agree that it is the human resources of a nation, not its capital or its material resources, that ultimately determine the character and pace of its economic and social development. For example, according to Professor Fredrick Harbison of Princeton University:

'Human resources . . . constitute the ultimate basis for wealth of nations. Capital and natural resources are passive factors of productions; human beings are the active agents who accumulate capital, exploit natural resources, build social, economic and political organizations, and carry forward national development. Clearly, a country which is unable to develop the skills and knowledge of its people and to utilize them effectively in the national economy will be unable to develop anything else.'[8]

Education, which is considered a right for every citizen, is viewed by the Omani government as a prime tool for rapidly developing the country's human resources. To this end, the government is heavily involved in education, exercising a strict control of the supply over educational services through direct provisions at all levels, and maintaining a strict regulatory framework for private education. As a result, educational expansion in Oman has been extraordinary (**Chart 4.4** and **Chart 4.5**).

In 1970, only 900 students were enrolled in primary schools (see Chapter One), but during the 1970s, average annual growth rates exceeded 60 per

Table 4.2

Evolution of Primary Education Enrolment Rates: Oman vs. Selected Countries (1970-90) (% rates)

Country	1970	1975	1980	1990
Egypt	72	75	89	97
Kuwait	89	92	102	100
Morocco	52	62	93	68
Tunisia	102	97	103	115
United Arab Emirates	98	101	88	111
Hong Kong	107	119	106	105
India	73	81	83	98
Indonesia	77	86	107	118
South Korea	103	107	110	108
Pakistan	40	119	106	105
Singapore	106	110	108	110
Argentina	106	106	106	111
Brazil	84	88	99	105
Ivory Coast	63	64	79	75
Kenya	61	104	115	94
Oman	3	44	60	102

Source: UNESCO, *Statistical Yearbooks* (1984, 1991).

Chart 4.4
Students in Government Schools (1986-93)

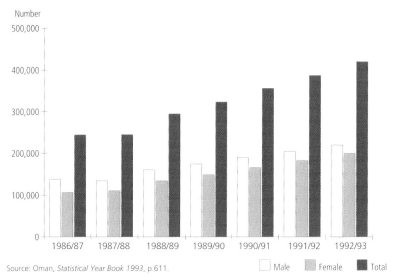

Source: Oman, *Statistical Year Book 1993*, p.611.

☐ Male   ▨ Female   ■ Total

Chart 4.5
Teachers in Government Schools (1985-93)

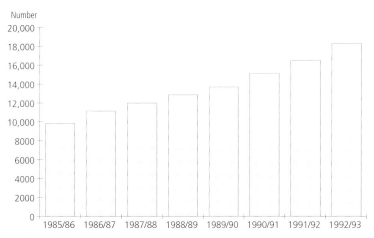

Source: Oman, *Statistical Year Book 1993*, p.611.

cent, and 13 per cent during the 1980s. As the development diamond indicates, Oman has made outstanding strides in education, whilst **Table 4.2** shows the evolution of primary enrolment in Oman compared with selected countries, demonstrating the uniqueness of Oman's expansion in education over the last 20 years. The gross enrolment ratio stood at 109 per cent in 1993, with the secondary enrolment ratio at 55 per cent (100% being the maximum enrolment confined to the primary age group).

As a testimony to Oman's achievement in education, as per Unicef's report,[9] Oman was ranked second in the league table of girls' education in the Middle East and North African Region, having achieved a 93 per cent rate of female children reaching at least grade 5 of primary school. Only six developing countries for whom data is available have achieved a higher percentage.

Comparing the actual level of progress in education with the expected level of its per capita GNP, 93 per cent of Omani children reach grade 5 of primary school, compared to the expected percentage of 92.[10] The

Chart 4.6
Primary and Secondary Enrolment Ratios in Schools: Oman vs. Medium and High Human Development Countries (1992)

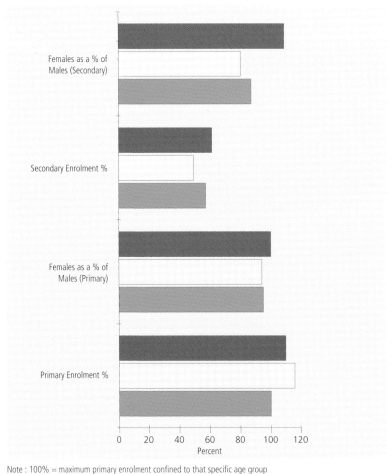

Note : 100% = maximum primary enrolment confined to that specific age group

■ Oman   ☐ Medium Human Development   ■ High Human Development

Source: UNDP, *Human Development Report* (1994).

remarkable progress achieved by Oman in primary and secondary enrolment ratios as compared to high and medium development countries is shown in **Chart 4.6**.

To achieve these remarkable improvements in education, the government has consistently allocated a substantial part of its recurrent expenditure budget to education. As **Chapter Annex Table 4.A.3** shows, the share of education in civil current expenditures (more than 23 per cent in 1991) indicates a faster growth rate in education expenditure than in other government sectors.

As a percentage of GDP, education expenditures represented 5.7 per cent in 1991, and grew regularly over the next three years. This ratio is not atypical, as public education represents from 4.1 to 7.3 per cent of GDP in industrial countries and from 2.5 to 7.5 per cent in developing countries.

As **Table 4.3** below shows, Oman's expenditure on education as a percentage of GDP was very high compared to the average expenditure in the major regions of the world. Likewise, public spending per capita was about RO 180 (US$460) – above the average level for developing countries, although well below that for industrialised countries (between US$500 and US$1,150 in OECD countries).

Table 4.3

Public Expenditure on Education by Major Regions (1987)

Regions	Public Expenditure on Education as Percentage of GNP	Public Expenditure on Education per Inhabitant (US$)
Africa (excluding Arab States)	4.8	15
Asia (excluding Arab States)	4.4	58
Arab States	6.6	134
Latin America and Caribbean	4.1	78
All Developed Countries	5.9	704
Oman	7.9	460

Source: UNESCO, *Statistical Yearbook* (1989).

4.3 Equality

Since data is not available about the pattern of income distribution and poverty levels, we shall use the accessibility to education as proxy for the measure of equality. 'The more equal an economy's distribution of income, the higher primary and secondary enrolments tend to be.'[11] The primary enrolment ratios achieved by Oman, as we have seen, are indeed very impressive, and with a growing population and free access to secondary education, enrolment ratios at secondary level are bound to increase considerably in the very near future.

In terms of equity in the allocation of education spending, the World Bank, in its Review of Recurrent Public Expenditure in Health and Education Sectors,[12] estimated a coefficient of dispersion (Gini coefficient) to measure the level of *vertical equity* in the distribution of public education spending among a generation of children. The result of the computation yielded a coefficient of 0.38 (**Chart 4.7**), a figure that indicates that the Omani educational system is more equitable in terms of age group, sex, class, and so on, than in most developing countries where the overall average is 0.60. This remains less equitable than that of industrial countries (Gini = 0.22).

Chart 4.7
Indicators of Vertical Equity in Education Expenditures: Oman vs. Selected Regions

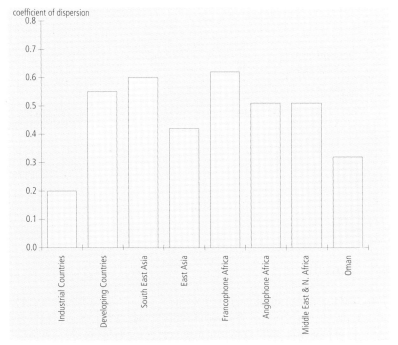

Note: The lower the ratio, the more equitable the distribution of public education expenditure.

Source: World Bank, *Oman: Review of Public Expenditure in Public Health and Education, August 1994*, p.50.

4.4 Employment

The human problems of developing countries are not confined to low levels of per capita income. Open unemployment in urban areas of developing countries is another dimension of the development problem, and an increasingly serious one.

However, since Oman started its demographic transition from Stage I[13] – stable or slow growing population – to Stage II – rapidly growing population – only in 1970, its available labour resources are hardly adequate for the explosion in demand for labour caused by the process of structural transformation of the economy, which was, as we discussed in earlier chapters, significantly influenced by oil revenues. Therefore, Oman has no unemployment problem. Whatever minor unemployment may exist, most of it is due to a mismatch of skills, and people waiting to get a public service job instead of joining the private sector (which employs about 85 per cent of the labour force).

Because of the rapid reduction in death rates and the continuing high birth rates, almost 52 per cent of Oman's population in 1990 was in the dependent age group (i.e. 1-15 years) (**Chart 4.8**). As a result, at the time of writing the number of people joining the labour market every year is hardly adequate to meet the growth in the economy.

Chart 4.8
Age Pyramid of Omani Population (1990)

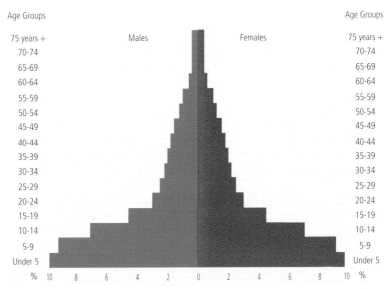

Source: Oman, *Fourth FYP* (1991), p.142a.

The total labour force grew by 50 per cent from 1975 to 1980, and by 70 per cent from 1980 to 1985. Because of the declining oil revenues it grew only by about 5 per cent between 1985 and 1990 (**Table 4.4**). In view of the enormous growth in the total labour force – which represents in Oman total demand for labour – the Omani labour market had to rely on expatriate labour. As a result, the share of Omani labour declined from 64.6 per cent in 1975 to 39.1 per cent in 1990.

Table 4.4

Estimate of Omani and Expatriate Labour Force (1975-90)

Year	Omani Labour		Expatriate Labour		Total Labour Force	
	Number (1,000s)	% of Total	Number (1,000s)	% of Total	Number (1,000s)	% of Total
1975	135	64.6	74	35.4	209	100.0
1980	152	49.7	154	50.3	306	100.0
1985	192	38.0	313	62.0	505	100.0
1990	207	39.1	322	60.9	529	100.0

Source: Oman, *Fourth FYP* (1991), p.146.

In terms of sectoral distribution of the labour force, in line with the Fisher-Clark[14] view, there has been a gradual shift of resources from agriculture to industry. As **Table 4.5** below shows, the proportion of the labour force engaged in agriculture, industry and services has been changing in line with the growth in GDP and the changing structure of the economy. The percentage of the labour force employed in agriculture dropped from 62 per cent in 1965 to 49 per cent in 1990-92, while the percentage employed in industry increased from 15 per cent to 22 per cent. The number employed in services increased from 23 per cent in 1965 to 29 per cent.

Table 4.5

Sectoral Distribution of Labour Force and GDP

	Agriculture	Industry	Services
Percentage of Labour Force (a)			
1965	62	15	23
1990-92	49	22	29
Relative Share of GDP (b)			
1970	16	77	7
1991	4	52	44

Source: UNDP, *Human Development Report* (1994); World Bank, *World Development Report* (1994).

Looking to the future, the greatest challenge facing the government will be setting appropriate education and training policies that will link the qualification and skills of the Omanis entering the labour force with the requirements of the labour market, and adopting pragmatic labour policies that will achieve optimum employment of Omanis and increase their participation in the labour force.

4.5 Conclusion

As we have seen in this chapter, although Oman did not specifically adopt a Basic Needs Approach to development – on the lines articulated by ILO, the World Bank,[15] and so on, – it did not rely on the 'trickle-down' effect of economic growth to achieve development.

While Oman's development strategy rightly stressed the need for growth and diversification, the government took it upon itself, through its Five-Year Plans, to achieve a wider distribution of the benefits of growth and to promote human development.

The remarkable results achieved in increased life expectancy, reduced infant mortality, universal access to primary education and almost full employment, clearly demonstrate the success of the policies adopted by the government in using the oil resources to achieve development through growth.

1   Hunt (1989), p.260.
2   Todaro (1992), p.87.
3   Hunt (1989), p.260.
4   Oman, *First FYP* (1976), pp.107–108.
5   Hunt (1989), p.269.
6.   UNICEF, *The Progress of Nations* (1994), p.50.
7   UNDP, *Human Development Report* (1994), p.152.
8   Todaro (1992), p.330.
9   UNICEF, *The Progress of Nations* (1994), p.20–21.
10   Ibid., p.48.
11   World Bank, *The East Asian Miracle* (1993), p.196.
12   World Bank, *Oman: Review of Recurrent Public Expenditure in Health and Education, August 1994* (1994), p.49.
13   Todaro (1992), pp.214–15.
14   Thirlwall (1990), pp.50–52.
15   Hunt (1989), pp.75–77.

Chapter Annex Table 4.A.1

The Hicks/Streeten List of Suggested Indicators of Basic Needs Performance

Need	Performance Indicator(s)
Health	Life expectancy at birth.
Education	Literacy; Primary school enrolment (as per cent of population aged 5-14).
Food	Calorie supply per head or calorie supply as per cent of requirements. *
Water Supply	Infant mortality (per thousand births); per cent of population with access to drinking water.
Sanitation	Infant mortality (per thousand births;** per cent of population with access to sanitation facilities.
Housing	None.

Notes:

* Since 1979, uncertainties among nutritionists as to calorie requirements have led the FAO to drop the per cent of required calories as a published indicator of nutritional levels and to refer simply to total calories available per head (see FAO, *Fifth World Food Survey,* 1985).

** The infant mortality rate is suggested as an indicator for both water supply and sanitation.

Source: Hunt, Diana, *Economic Theories of Development,* (1989) p.269.

Chapter Annex Table 4.A.2

Development of Health Services (1971-90)

Year	No. of In-Patients	Indice of Growth (1971 = 100)	No. of Hospital Beds	Indice of Growth (1971 = 100)	No. of Out-Patients	
1971	3,974	100	216	100	56,098	
1972	12,430	313	526	244	120,380	
1973	23,140	582	664	307	145,110	
1974	28,800	725	934	432	183,330	
1975	56,119	1,412	1,000	463	1,376,580	
1976	64,900	1,633	1,252	580	1,982,000	
1977	77,700	1,955	1,409	652	2,449,300	
1978	86,431	2,175	1,409	652	2,564,317	
1979	92,462	2,327	1,428	661	2,777,400	
1980	108,208	2,723	1,784	826	3,123,354	
1981	125,608	3,161	1,866	864	2,525,854	
1982	134,999	3,397	2,041	945	3,328,434	
1983	142,722	3,591	2,133	988	3,616,137	
1984	155,546	3,914	2,587	1,198	4,071,611	
1985	150,798	3,795	2,813	1,302	4,589,863	
1986	151,868	3,822	2,841	1,315	4,821,734	
1987	166,611	4,193	3,450	1,597	5,296,596	
1988	177,470	4,466	3,316	1,535	5,435,136	
1989	177,338	4,462	3,360	1,556	5,591,425	
1990	183,375	4,614	3,431	1,588	5,837,768	
Average Annual Rate of Growth (%) 1971-80 39.16			23.51		49.47	
Average Annual Rate of Growth (%) 1981-90 3.86			6.28		8.74	
Average Annual Rate of Growth (%) 1971-90 22.34			15.67		83.53	

Source: Oman, *Statistical Year Book 1990* pp.522 and 539.

Indice of Growth (1971 = 100)	No. of Doctors	Indice of Growth (1971 = 100)	No. of Nurses	No. of Growth (1971 = 100)
100	46	100	77	100
215	61	133	115	149
259	84	183	208	270
327	150	326	335	435
2,454	147	320	411	534
3,533	160	348	522	678
4,366	202	439	624	810
4,571	208	452	659	856
4,951	215	467	687	892
5,568	294	639	857	1,113
4,503	348	757	1,025	1,331
5,933	385	837	1,164	1,512
6,446	465	1,011	1,386	1,800
7,258	572	1,213	1,753	2,277
8,182	638	1,387	1,947	2,529
8,595	674	1,465	2,057	2,671
9,442	836	1,817	2,973	3,861
9,689	907	1,972	3,260	4,234
9,967	919	1,998	3,274	4,252
10,406	994	2,161	3,512	4,561
	20.38		27.25	
	11.07		13.11	
	17.56		22.27	

Chapter Annex Table 4.A.3

Breakdown of Civil Current Expenditure (1978, 1988-91)
(In Million RO)

Details of Expenditure	1978	Share (%)	1988	Share (%)	1989	Share (%)	1990	Share (%)	1991	Share (%)
General Public Sector	99.6	20.0	86.1	16.1	102.6	17.0	118.9	18.1	110.9	16.4
Education Affairs & Services	111.2	22.0	118.0	22.0	128.2	21.4	153.9	23.3	160.9	23.9
Health	51.8	10.0	61.4	11.5	63.4	10.6	69.5	10.5	75.6	11.2
Housing	48.2	9.6	55.1	10.3	58.9	10.0	72.2	10.9	100.2	14.9
Fuel and Energy	89.7	18.0	96.0	18.0	97.0	16.0	104.3	15.8	76.8	11.4
Agriculture Forestry & Fisheries	11.7	2.3	12.5	2.3	13.0	2.2	16.5	2.5	19.2	2.8
Transportation & Communication	19.1	3.8	21.9	4.1	21.4	3.6	23.5	3.6	23.5	3.5
Other	68.2	14.3	84.2	15.7	115.5	19.3	101.2	15.3	107.0	15.9
Total Civil Current Expenditure	499.5	100.0	535.2	100.0	600.0	100.0	660.0	100.0	674.1	100.0

Source: Oman, *Statistical Year Books.*

Chapter Five

Overall Assessment and Conclusion

We began this study with the objective of understanding the role and impact of oil revenues on the transformation of a traditional economy. We found that with the benefit of a wise and dedicated leadership, increased level of oil revenues, and appropriate policies, Oman has developed at a rapid pace since HM Sultan Qaboos bin Said assumed power in July, 1970. Then it was a typical underdeveloped country with only 10 kms. of paved roads, three schools and 12 hospital beds serving 666,000 people across a territory of 309,000 sq. kms. and with a traditional large agricultural sector. Oman's physical infrastructure has been brought up to advanced, modern standards over much of the country. Basic health indicators reveal dramatic improvements in life expectancy and sharp reductions in infant mortality. The coverage of primary education has become almost universal. Twenty per cent of boys and girls now attend secondary schools and a growing number of students in a widening range of fields are graduating from Sultan Qaboos University.

In the final chapter of this study, we will attempt to analyse the perspectives that have guided Oman's development strategy over the last two decades and conclude with an assessment of the challenges that lie ahead.

5.1 Oman's development perspectives

In order to analyse and understand Oman's development perspectives, it is important to point out that at the time Oman embarked on its development crusade with the launch of its First FYP (1976-80) in 1976, the whole discipline of development economics was under attack. On the one hand, there were an increasing number of economists, such as Seers,[1] arguing for the 'dethronement' of GNP and the elevation of direct attacks on widespread absolute poverty, increasingly inequitable income distributions, and rising unemployment. In short, there were growing calls for a redefinition of development. On the other hand, the neo-classical counter-revolution[2] was calling for the dismantling of public ownership, planning, and regulation of economic activities in developing countries.

While the debates of the 1970s continued, Oman launched its development strategy in the firm belief that the circumstances – economic, political and social – of each underdeveloped economy vary, and that the appropriate path of economic and political development cannot be determined *a priori*, but only in the context of its specific conditions. At the same time, as we have seen, Oman was very eclectic in the strategies and policies it adopted for economic development, the principal features and characteristics of which were:

1 Oman's development strategy which, while emphasising the important role of the market in the development process, gave the public sector a dominant role in accelerating economic development.

2 In line with the neo-classical theory of trade and development, and by using its primary commodity – oil – as the leading sector of the economy, the government was able to vent a surplus through trade, which was then used to carry out a massive investment programme to achieve economic expansion and structural diversification.

3 Despite the negative attitudes prevailing towards multinationals in the 1970s , which led to a spate of nationalisation by a number of oil producing developing countries, Oman embraced the tenets of neo-classical theory in dealing with oil multinationals. As a result, multinationals not only contributed about 50 per cent of the investments required in the oil sector over the period 1976-92, but they also brought with them modern technology and management expertise which were instrumental in increasing daily oil production from 366,000 b/d in 1976 to 780,000 barrels a day in 1993, while, at the same time, increasing the level of reserves during the same period from 1,280 million barrels to about 4,735 million barrels, as we saw in Chapter Two.

4 Within the framework of a long-term development strategy, which was implemented through a series of Five-Year Plans from 1976 onwards, the government was able to achieve an annual average growth rate of 8 per cent per annum between 1972 and 1992 – one of the highest in the world. At the same time, GNP grew at an average rate of more than 6 per cent per

annum between 1965 aand 1990 (see Chapter Three).

5 In line with the arguments articulated in Chapter Three about the importance of savings and capital formation for achieving economic development, the government – directly through fiscal policy and indirectly through the private sector – was able to generate average annual savings of about 46.7 per cent of GDP during 1976-81; and although the rate of savings declined to about 31.3 per cent on average during 1986-91, these rates of savings were nevertheless higher than the ones suggested by Rostow for the 'take-off' stage. As a result, the government was able to achieve a structural transformation of the economy through an ambitious and sometimes unbalanced investment programme. Whereas oil and gas, representing primary output in 1970, accounted for almost 70 per cent of GDP at factor cost, its relative share stood at 49 per cent in 1990 and declined further to 38 per cent of GDP in 1993. Meanwhile, the agriculture, fisheries and manufacturing share in the GDP rose from 2.6 per cent in 1976 to 7.1 per cent in 1990 and to 8.5 per cent in 1993.[3]

6 As discussed in Chapter Three, pragmatic orthodoxy in macro-economic management, in line with the tenets of the neo-classical paradigm, was also one of the important contributing factors to the achievement of real growth and economic development.

7 Although Oman's development plans emphasised the importance of growth in achieving economic development, these plans, and the development strategy within which they were formulated, did not rely on the 'trickle-down' mechanism to achieve human development. In fact, people were and are the forefront of the Omani development process. As a result, and as we have seen in Chapter Four, life expectancy has increased rapidly from 49 years in 1972 to 67.1 years in 1993, and infant mortality has declined from 64 per thousand in 1980 to 23 per thousand in 1993. In education, the number of schools has jumped from three in 1969 to 1,002 in 1993, while the number of students has exploded from 900 in 1969 to 481,071 in 1993.

5.2 The importance of 'political will'

One important feature, and perhaps the most significant one, of Oman's development experience has been the 'political will' and commitment on the part of HM Sultan Qaboos to reform and development. Waterston summarises his analysis of the development planning thus:

'The available evidence makes it clear that in countries with development plans, lack of adequate government support for the plans is the prime reason why most are never carried out. Conversely, the cardinal lesson that emerges from the planning experience of developing countries is that the sustained commitment of a politically stable government is the *sine qua non* for development. Where a country's political leadership makes development a central concern, the people can also be interested through a judicious use of economic incentives. And, although it is never easy to reform administrative and institutional inefficiency, commitment by political leaders is a necessary condition for reform; without it, reform is impossible.'[4]

5.3 Future challenges

Oman enters the twenty-first century with a remarkable record of social and economic achievements, and a long and successful experience in development management. One should not underestimate the challenges that lie ahead if continued sustainable growth, increased industrial diversification and enhanced efficiency are to be achieved. Therefore, Oman's future development strategy should focus on a number of issues including:

1 Eliminating public sector deficits which, because of declining oil revenues and growing public expenditure, have been a regular feature of the government budgets since 1986 (**Chapter Annex Table 3.A.1**).

2 Generating and maintaining a high rate of public saving which should be invested in high income-yielding assets that could eventually replace oil revenues.

3 Strengthening the existing mechanisms to insulate the economy from the effects of the 'Dutch disease' in periods of high oil prices and from the adverse terms of trade in periods of low prices.

4 Expanding and strengthening the role of the private sector in the economy and thereby reducing its reliance on public expenditure.

5 Improving the educational and vocational training systems to enhance Omanis' skills and adaptability to a changing international environment, and to be better equipped to participate effectively in the economy.

GOD BLESS US ALL

1   Todaro (1992), p.87.
2   Ibid., p.82.
3   Oman, *Statistical Year Books*.
4   Hunt (1989), p.320.

Appendix I

Royal Decree No. 6/1991
For Approving the Administrative Structure of the Sultanate

We, Qaboos bin Sa'id, Sultan of Oman,

After perusal of the Royal Decree No.26/75 for the issue of the Law of The State Administrative Board and its amendments;

And for activating the civil and economic movement in the Country;

And for facilitating the distribution of services around all cities and villages of the Sultanate;

And for facilitating the selection of the *Wilayats'* Representatives in the Parliament;

And for the public interest;

Have decided the following:

Article 1: The Administrative Structure shall be approved according to the appendix attached.

Article 2: All departments concerned should process the amendments needed onto their interior regulations as per the said Administrative Structure.

Article 3: This Decree shall be published in the Official Gazette and comes into force on the date of its issue.

Qaboos bin Said
Sultan of Oman

Issued on: 17 Ragab 1411
3 February 1991

Administrative Regions and *Wilayats*

Region	*Wilayat* (district)	Region	*Wilayat* (district)
1 Muscat (Capital)	Muscat Seeb Muttrah Baushar Al-Amrat Quriyat	5 A'Dakhliyah	Nizwa Samail Bahla Adam Al-Hamra Manah Izki
2 Al-Batinah	Sohar A'Rustaq Shinas Liwa Saham Al-Khabourah A'Suwaiq Nakhal Wadi Al-Ma'awil Al-Awabi Al-Masna'ah Barka	6 A'Sharqiyah	Bidbid Sur Ibra Biddiya Al-Qabil Al-Mudhaibi Dima Wa A'Tayeen Al-Kamil wa al-Wafi Jalan Bani Bu Ali Jalan Bani Bu Hassan Wadi Bani Khalid Masirah
3 Musandam	Khasab Bukha Diba Al-Bayah Madha	7 Al-Wusta	Haima Muhut A'Duqm Al-Jazer
4 A'Dhahirah	Al-Buraimi Ibri Mahadha Yankul Dhank	8 Dhofar	Salalah Thumrait Taqah Mirbat Sadah Rakhyut Dhalkut Muqshin Al-Halaniyat

Appendix II

The Word of Sultan Sa'id bin Taimur, Sultan of Muscat and Oman, about the history of the financial position of the Sultanate in the past and the hope for the future, and after the export of oil.

We consider the first period to run from pre-1914 to 1920. The Government in the era of our grandfather, Sultan Faisal bin Turki, and in the era before him, had only a simple way of despatching all the affairs of the country; no budget, no planning and no organisation. Improvisation was the basis of all that was done and said. This was the situation prevailing at that time in most Arab countries.

In 1913 (1331) our beloved father, Sultan Tamur bin Faisal, succeeded to the throne on the death of Sultan Faisal bin Turki. He inherited a legacy of many debts and a Government burdened with loans due to be repaid to the merchants of the country. This situation continued and the debts increased until 1920, when, realising it was not easy to rule the country with its finances in such a state of weakness and disorganisation, he determined to introduce modern methods. It was clear that his Government could make little progress until it was freed of its burden of debts to the merchants. He realised that it would be best to negotiate one major loan which would enable him to liquidate the old debts yet still leave a surplus which could be used to achieve the desired reforms. The only body able to meet his request was the Government of British India, which agreed to lend him the necessary money on the understanding that it would be repaid in ten years. He decided at the same time to ask the Egyptian Government for officials to reorganise the Customs. The Egyptian Government agreed and sent him three Customs experts who set about their work with a will. He also engaged an English official, Mr D.V. McCullum, to supervise the reorganisation of the Finance Department.

Thereafter the finances of the Government slowly recovered; there were no deficits in the annual budgets and the loan instalments were paid off regularly.

The English official engaged in 1920 stayed for only six months, however, and, in the absence of a successor, Sultan Taimur appointed Mohammed bin Ahmed al Ghashan, then Wali of Matrah, as Minister responsible for financial affairs. This situation prevailed until the end of 1924, when there was a deficit due to the negligence of the officer responsible and the maladministration of the Treasury Officer, as a result of which the State finances were so shaken as to make it impossible to continue to repay the loan instalments on time.

The second period begins in 1925 when, in view of the poor state of Government finances, Sultan Taimur bin Faisal decided to engage a new official to reorganise them. He appointed an Englishman, Mr Bertram Thomas, as Finance Minister on a five-year contract, with a view to his improving the Government's financial position. (Mr Thomas was the first Westerner to cross the Empty Quarter, doing so from Dhofar to Qatar in 54 days.) At the outset he exerted considerable efforts which produced a measure of improvemenmt. Unfortunately this improvement was maintained for only three years, after which the financial situation again deteriorated and the Government ceased to repay the instalments of the loan. This was due to the maladministration of the official in respect of the previous period, in allowing the Government spending to exceed the approved Budget. This led to a deficit and disorder in State finances. The balance of payments was upset: unpaid instalments of the loan, and other expenditure, piled up, constituting a new debt, additional to the balance of the previous one.

In 1930 an economic slump struck the world. This affected the trade balance, resulting in a sharp fall in Customs revenues, which were virtually the Government's only source of revenue. While great hopes were pinned on Mr Thomas to repair what others had destroyed, he in fact brought the finances to ruin and left them in an even sorrier state.

Thereafter Sultan Taimur bin Faisal considered engaging a financial expert to put right what was wrong. In 1930 he engaged as his Financial Adviser Mr Hedgecock, an Englishman and a senior official of the Iraqi Finance Ministry, who immediately set to work with great vigour and determination to rescue the finances from the state they were in as a result of Bertram Thomas's maladministration. He reduced salaries and cut expenditure and was eventually able to put the financial records in order and to organise proper Budgets. We reveal no secrets if we say that at that time the Government's Budget was no more than Rupees 700,000 (Pounds Sterling 50,000) from which the Sultanate had to pay the cost of the Government machine, repay the balance of the loan and meet various other items of expenditure, including the customary gifts and presents to the tribal Sheikhs and delegations, since, outwardly, the Government appeared very rich. Mr Hedgecock deserves admiration and respect for what he did to reorganise the finances of the

Sultanate. Unfortunately however he did not stay long, resigning for private reasons after eight months.

At that time we were Prime Minister with oversight of the Sultanate's financial affairs. After the resignation of Mr Hedgecock it was decided to appoint Mr R.J. Alban, an Englishman, as Financial Adviser. And then on 2 Shawal 1350 (11 February 1932), we succeeded to power upon the abdication, for reasons of health, of our beloved father, Sultan Taimur bin Faisal.

We gave our special attention to finance but found that because of the effects of economic pressure on world trade we were compelled to reduce expenditure in various sectors, our first economy being to halve the Sultan's Privy Purse. The reader may be surprised to learn that when we took over the reins of power the Sultanate's Treasury was completely empty. No doubt many of our contemporaries will recall what the financial situation was like in those days.

However, thanks to painstaking efforts and close supervision of finances, signs of improvement became visible, and, as 1933 neared its end, debts had been liquidated and the sums due to the merchants paid off. At the end of 1933 the Financial Adviser resigned, whereupon we assumed complete personal control of the Sultanate's finances and the preparation of its annual Budgets. The improvement in Customs revenues continued (the Sultanate having no other income to speak of) enabling us to raise officials' salaries and to give attention to the welfare of the Sultanate. The financial position has continued to improve until the present day.

The third period runs from1939, with the outbreak of the Second World War, until 1945. During this period prices rose and consequently, so too did Customs revenues. We further increased officials' salaries and undertook much needed reforms in various parts of the Sultanate. From 1933 to this day there has been no financial deficit in the Government's Budget and the Government has been able to build up reasonable financial reserves against emergencies, as well as meeting necessary expenditure in various fields, especially that of defence, which swallowed up about half the Budget. We were anxious to introduce various urgently needed reforms for the welfare of the country, but found that there was not enough leeway either in the Budget or in the reserves to support any sort of planning, for we did not want to overburden the Sultanate's finances and weigh them down with new debts, having paid off all the old ones. Doubtless it would have been easy to obtain money in various ways, but this could only have been a loan with interest at a set percentage rate. This amounts to usury, with which I completely disagree, and the religious prohibition of which is not unknown.

By now the financial position of the Sultanate will have been made plain to you by the facts we have set out, and which account for the inability of Government of the time to bring the country up-to-date. We were fully aware of the many reforms which the country needed, but whilst the eyesight was long, the arm at that time was short. Despite all this, however, we were never at a loss to undertake any work which brought general benefit to the country whenever we found a way to do so. For example, when the opportunity occurred in 1940, during the War, we built the Saidiya School in Muscat, the first Government building constructed after getting over the difficult period. Similarly we made a number of improvements to Government centres and forts in various *Wilayats*.

In 1958 our friends, the British Government, offered us financial assistance to strengthen the Sultanate's Army; to introduce improvements in education; to set up Health Centres in some of the *Wilayats* along the coast and in the interior; to build Experimental Farms to raise the standard of farming in the country; to construct roads and other improvements. We accepted with deep gratitude. There was a time limit to it in that it was to continue only until the finances of the Sultanate improved. It continued until the end of March last year, i.e. four months before oil exports began at the end of July 1967. During this interim period we depended upon such financial reserves as we had. Had it not been for our economy and for our reserves, we would not have been able to bear the burden of expenditure during these months. In particular, the allocation to the Sultanate Army took up a large part of our resources until the Government obtained its share of oil revenues.

Now the oil flows from the fields at Fahud and Natih through the pipes to the tanks at Mina al Fahl in Saih al Maleh (which ought now to be called Saih al Huluw). Soon the product of another field at Jibal near Fahud will flow to join the output of the first two fields supplying the tanks at Saih al Huluw, whence the oil is pumped out to the tankers anchored at Mina al Fahl to be carried away. Thus our dear country becomes among the exporters of oil, and we can insert a new sub-heading in our Budget: 'Oil Revenues'. Yes, only now that we know that revenue from oil will be coming in steadily can we consider and plan and estimate how to put into effect the various projects which the country needs. We hope these revenues will continue to increase each year.

We ought at this stage to mention the relationship between the Sultanate and the oil company. The first agreement was concluded in the middle of 1937. The Company paid a rent for the right to search for oil in Sultanate territory and this helped strengthen the Budget somewhat. In 1964, when oil was discovered in commercial quantities in the Sultanate, the present Company suggested a revision of the agreement signed between the Sultanate and the previous oil company, the new agreement to correspond with similar agreements signed recently between various oil companies and the Governments of the oil exporting countries of the Middle East. The Sultanate agreed and asked the Company to put forward a suggested revision for the

Government to study.

In March 1967, after talks between the Sultanate and the Company, Agreements were concluded giving the Government 50 per cent of the oil profits, and the right to 12.5 per cent of all oil exported. This accorded with the decision of OPEC, an organisation formed of some of the Middle East oil exporting countries. The Agreement included many other matters bringing advantage and general benefit to the country.

All this took place during the period in which Mr F. Hughes was the Company's General Manager and Representative. He was appointed by the Company to negotiate the detailed revision of the Agreement and we found a complete understanding of the situation on his part. Agreement on terms was reached with great ease, thanks to the efforts displayed by him so that the Agreement should benefit both sides.

God willing, 1968 will be the start of a new era for our country which will see the beginning of various plans which will be executed under the supervision of qualified technicians and experts. Firstly we shall begin building offices for various Government Departments; then houses for officials who will come from abroad; then step by step will come various projects such as hospitals, schools, roads, communications, and other necessary works including the development of fisheries, animal husbandry and agricultural resources, etc., until modern projects have spread over the whole of the Sultanate, to each area according to its needs. So long as oil flows the Government will match its flow with continuing development for the welfare of the country. Naturally projects involve much effort and hard work. The progress we see in other countries was not the work of a day, but the result of efforts over long years. It takes time for the results of projects for improvement to be seen and there will be an unavoidable gap between the receipt of oil revenues and the appearance of benefits for the populace. We are straining every nerve to improve the lot of the country both in general and in particular.

An initial task is to increase the salaries of Government officials which we consider need to be increased and to establish a cadre to regularise promotion. We shall reinforce the Government machine by adding to it a number of experts and technicians. This will ensure that the Government has a modern administrative machine. The present situation requires changes in the existing Government set-up.

There are urgent schemes to which we consider we must give priority:

1 Water – Work on this project is being pressed ahead, and we hope that a water pipeline to Muscat and Muttrah will be laid within 21 months of the date of contract, making pure water available to all.

2 Electricity – All the preliminary stages have been completed and work is going ahead briskly. It is hoped that the Company to which the project has been entrusted will supply electricity to consumers in Muscat and Muttrah next summer.

3 Muttrah Port – Because of Muttrah's outstanding natural location, secure commercial position and reliable communications with the various parts of the Sultanate, which make it the commercial capital of the country, we consider that we should make a start on the construction of port facilities in the near future, to which the general Customs Department will be transferred, and where steamers, sailing crafts and motor boats may moor to load and discharge. Sufficient warehouses will be provided for the storage and protection of incoming and outgoing goods.

4 Saidi currency - Another project which will be given priority and special study is that of currency. The Saidi currency will be based on the Saidi Riyal, sub-divided into ½ Riyal and ¼ Riyal. Baizas will be minted to meet the requirements of the people, denominations being of 100, 25, 20, 10, 5 and 1 Baiza. The necessary announcement about this will be made at the appropriate time.

When we talk about planning we must not forget the oil-bearing area and the Duru tribe who live there. They must be given special attention and must get the projects they need and which suit them.

Other plans will follow later, in order of importance. We must not forget that the area of the Sultanate is more than 100,000 square miles, that its coastline is no less than 1,000 miles long and that its population is estimated at more than half a million.

We shall appoint a body, known as the Development Board, to execute such plans as we decide upon. This body will be responsible for drawing up a Budget for each project and for keeping in touch with experts, technicians and others whom it is necessary to consult in connection with any desired project.

We shall also appoint a special Board for the water and electricity schemes. It will oversee the progress of work and will ensure that the schemes conform with the regulations fixed by the Government to safeguard the needs of the people.

We are now passing through a preliminary planning stage for the projects which enjoy priority because they are for the benefit of all. We are looking forward to a bright future by which we guarantee raising the standard of living of the inhabitants of the Sultanate and increasing the income of the individual. We shall develop the country so as to keep pace with the cavalcade of present-day civilisation. We shall ensure every benefit and advantage for the populace and we shall pursue those developments which bring us that which is best and preferable and is consonant with our people's heritage and ancient history. However much we progress and move forward, we must keep before our eyes our true religion on which we place our reliance, and on the traditions which are our heritage. There are prohibitions in our religion which are inviolable for ever; and there are customs which can be altered without infringing the basic traditions of the country which are among the glories of our worthy ancestors, a source of pride and a protection of our very existence. The Almighty said in his Book 'Say "work" and God will see your work'.

We ask the Almighty whose works are great to inspire us to do that which is right, to crown our efforts with success, bring us success in our enterprise and grant us victory in our desires. We are humble towards him whose power is sublime and brings us success in what is for the good of our Omani people and our country.

Published: January 1968

Appendix III

Press Release Issued by HM Sultan Qaboos, 26 July 1970

Fellow countryman. I speak to you as Sultan of Muscat and Oman having succeeded my father on the 24th of July 1970, 19 of Jamada al Uwla 1390. I have watched with growing dismay and increasing anger the inability of my father to use the new found wealth of this country for the needs of its people. That is why I have taken control. My family and my armed forces have pledged their loyalty to me. The ex-Sultan has left the Sultanate.

I promise you all that my immediate task will be to set up as quickly as possible a forceful and modern government whose first aim must be to remove unnecessary restrictions under which you, my people, now suffer, and to produce as rapidly as possible a happier and more secure future for all of you.

I ask the help of each one of you in this task. In days gone by our country was great and powerful, and with God's help, if we work together to recreate our nation we shall once again take our rightful place in the Arab world.

I am taking the necessary constitutional steps to receive recognition from foreign countries with whom we have relations, and I look forward to the early establishment of friendly cooperation with all nations, notably with our neighbours, and to an era of active consultation with them on the future of the region.

My friends, I urge you to continue with your normal lives, knowing that I will be coming to Muscat within a very short period, and that my major concern will be to tell you, Oh my people, what I and my new government plan to do to achieve our common aim. My friends, my brothers, yesterday was dark, but with God's help, tomorrow will dawn bright for Muscat and Oman and all its people.

May God's blessing be upon us and on our endeavours.

Appendix IV

Members of the First Joint Management Committee, 1974

Mr Salem H. Macki:	Director of Petroleum and Minerals
Mr Mohamed Musa Al-Yousef:	Director of Treasury and Accounts
Mr Lord Gorell:	Shell
Mr J. van der Eijk:	Shell
Mr J.P. Brousseau:	CFP
Mr. R.Gulbenkian:	Partex
Mr. R Jackli:	Chief Executive of the Operating Company
Dr Y. Nimatallah:	Adviser to the Government
Mrs J.S. Jennings:	Exploration Manager (PDO)
Mr. W. Mathieu:	Production Manager (PDO)
Mr. G. Searle:	Finance Manager (PDO)

Appendix V

Royal Decree No.1/1980*
Creating the State General Reserve Fund

We, Qaboos bin Said, Sultan of Oman,

In accordance with the targets and policies of the Second Five-Year Plan;

In order to ensure the feature of the economic development of the Sultanate;

With reference to the Royal Decree No. 26/1975, as amended, issuing the law on the organisation of the government administration;

With reference to the Royal Decree number 48/1976 concerning the authorisation to sign, on behalf of the government, internal and external transactions;

And in accordance with public interest;

Have decreed the following:

Article One
A State General Reserve Fund is hereby established as a separate financial and legal entity.

Article Two
The Financial Affairs Council shall supervise the SGRF and shall be responsible for ensuring the soundness of its operations and of its financial position.

Article Three
The Directorate General of Finance shall be the executive agency of the SGRF and shall be responsible for maintaining its accounts and implementing the policies and decisions taken by the Financial Affairs Council regarding the investment and disbursement of the assets of the SGRF.

The Directorate General of Finance shall present to the Financial Affairs Council monthly reports giving the details of the SGRF financial position and its receipts and expenses.

Article Four
The Financial Affairs Council shall decide the policies and regulations governing the investment of the assets of the SGRF and shall amend such policies and regulations in accordance with the requirements of changing economic conditions.
The Financial Affairs Council shall, in particular, decide on the following:

1 To nominate the banks and other financial institutions with which or through which the assets of the SRGF may be invested, as well as the maximum amounts of money that may be invested with or through each of these banks and institutions.

2 To determine the convertible currencies in which the SGRF may hold its assets and the maximum amount that may be held in each of these currencies.

3 To determine the types of bonds or stocks in which the SGRF may invest its assets.

4 To approve any agreement or contract between the SGRF and any other parties.

5 The Financial Affairs Council may consult with the Central Bank of Oman in the carrying-out of the provisions mentioned above.

Article Five

The assets of the SGRF shall not be invested except in negotiable assets valued in converted currencies, in the form of gold, deposits, or stocks and bonds issued by governments, government institutions, or private institutions with sound financial positions.

Article Six

There shall be no withdrawals from the SGRF except for the purpose of financing a deficit in the state budget in the years which may require such withdrawals and by a decision of the Financial Affairs Council in each case, or for the purpose of meeting SGRF expenses or financial obligations within the rules of this Decree.

Article Seven

The SGRF assets may be used for guaranteeing Government loans by a decision from the Financial Affairs Council in each case.

Article Eight

The resources of the SGRF shall be composed of the following:

1 All Government liquid or negotiable assets which are valued in convertible currencies and which represent a surplus in the Government finances on 1 January 1980, except for the operating accounts necessary for the functioning of the government.

2 Fifteen percent of each sum received from net oil revenues.

3 Any surplus from the investment of the SGRF assets.

4 The income from the investment of the SGRF assets.

5 Any other monies we decree to add to the assets of the SGRF.

Article Nine

The Financial Affairs Council is hereby authorised to issue by-laws for the SGRF within the rules of this Decree.

Article Ten

The authorisation to sign on behalf of the SGRF shall be subject to the Royal Decree No.48/1976 concerning the authorisation to sign, on behalf of the Government, internal and external transactions.

Article Eleven
This Decree shall be published in the Official Gazette and shall be enforced as of 1 January 1980.

Qaboos bin Said
Sultan of Oman

Issued on: 17 Safar, 1400
     6 January 1980

* Unofficial translation.

Appendix VI

Royal Decree No. 1/1991*
Ratification of the Fourth Five-Year Development Plan (1991-95)

We, Qaboos bin Said, Sultan of Oman,

After perusal of the Royal Decree No.26/1975 issuing the Law of Organisation of the Government Administrative Body as amended;

The Economic Development Law, 1975;

The Royal Decree No.1/1980 establishing the State General Reserve Fund;

With due concern about the Plan's comprehensiveness to cover all regions of the Sultanate;

With an intention to augment development programmes and accomplish higher rates of growth in the non-oil production sectors in order to diversify the sources of income;

To emphasise the development of the national labour force to enhance its participation in the economy; and,

In accordance with the exigencies of the public interest;

Have decreed as follows:

Article I: The Fourth Five-Year Development Plan (1991–95) as summarised in the appended table, is hereby endorsed.

Article II: The principles appended to this Decree shall be complied with in the implementation of the Plan.

Article III: The Development Council shall publish the details of the Fourth Five-Year Development Plan in special reports to be issued to this end.

Article IV: All ministries and government agencies shall implement the aforesaid Fourth Five-Year Development Plan without prejudice to the Tender Rules or the regulations governing the approval of the State's annual budget and measures of implementation thereof.

Article V: This Decree shall be published in the Offical Gazette and shall take effect as from 1 January 1991.

Qaboos bin Said
Sultan of Oman

Issued on: Jumada II, 1411
          1 January 1991

* Unofficial translation.

Principle of the Fourth Five-Year Plan

1 The system of transfer of a proportion of net oil revenues to the State General Reserve Fund shall be continued in accordance with Article I of Royal Decree No.1/1980, establishing the State General Reserve Fund. The transfer proportion shall be raised from 5 per cent to 15 per cent of every net payment of oil revenues as stated in para (2) Article 8, in the aforesaid Decree.

2 A Contingency Fund shall be established to receive 7.5 per cent of the net oil revenues if oil prices range between US$18–20 per barrel and 10 per cent if the price per barrel exceeds US$20 and up to US$22, to cope with any international or domestic variables that might emerge during the Plan's implementation.

3 An additional sum of RO 150 million shall be allocated for the civil development expenditure throughout the years 1993-95 and be effected within the annual budgets in accordance with the distribution approved by the Cabinet. The Development Council shall provide the said sum during the years 1991-92 from the following sources:

a Available additional funds if higher oil prices are realised above the assumed levels.

b The Contingency Fund.

c By the adjustment of the investment expenditure if the implementation of the development projects is below the assumed percentage.

4 The annual growth rate of civil recurrent expenditure shall not exceed 3.5 per cent during the Plan period.

5 The deficit between total revenue and total expenditure shall not exceed a maximum of 10 per cent of total revenue.

6 The external public debt shall remain at its level at the end of the Third Five-Year Plan. Additional net external borrowing shall not be resorted to without the Cabinet's decision.

7 Any increase above the oil prices assumed in the calculation of the appended table and up to the price of US$25 per barrel, shall be distributed to the different uses as per ratios approved by the Cabinet. Any further increase in prices shall be transferred to the State General Reserve Fund.

8 If actual net oil revenue falls during the Plan period below the estimated average prices, some items of expenditure shall be reconsidered to match the rate of decline in international prices, such that the provisions of paras (5) and (6) in this appendix are complied with.

9 Upon the ratification of the Integrated General Strategy, concerned agencies shall reassess the Plan, to the extent necessary for the present Plan period.

Appendix Table VII.1

Social Indicators (1970-93)

	Indicators	1970	1971	1975	1980
1	Population			1,085,757	1,250,831
2	GNP per Capita (Omani Rial)			667	1,480
3	HEALTH INDICATORS				
a	Crude Death Rate				13.3
b	Life Expectancy at Birth (Year)				57.5
c	Infant Mortality per 1,000 Live Births				64.0
d	Children Immunisation Coverage (%)				
e	Population per Physician			7,386	2,410
f	Population per Nurse			2,525	1,279
g	Population per Hospital Bed			911	587
h	Population per Dentist			180,960	52,118
i	Population per Pharmacist			16,704	26,613
j	Birth Rates per 1,000 Population				50.0
4	EDUCATION INDICATORS				
a	Schools & Institutes	16	45	214	412
b	Classes	151	345	1,621	3,658
c	Students	6,941	15,334	56,264	111,771
d	Teachers	196	445	2,230	5,458
e	College Students (inside & outside)			374	939
f	Students per Class	45.97	44.45	34.71	30.56
g	Students per Teacher	35.41	34.46	25.23	20.48
5	Manpower (Government Sector)	1,750	3,112	19,123	40,340
6	% Omani	93.14	91.81	71.20	60.86
7	Roads Asphalted (Km.)	10	27	714	2192
8	Telephone Lines (no.)	557	989	3,701	15,044
9	Electricity Production/Million Kw per Hour	8	13	154	818
10	Electricity Consumption/Million Kw per Hour	7	12	146	730
11	Water Production/Million Gallons	14.0	85.0	35,805.0	3001.2
12	Water Consumption/Million Gallons	9.0	629.0	276.5	2074.8

Source: Oman, *Statistical Year Books*.

1984	1985	1988	1989	1990	1991	1992	1993
1,449,476	1,503,936	1,682,444	1,746,377	1,812,739	1,879,810	1,949,364	2,017,591
1,860	2,031	1,497	1,619	2,003	1,859	1,972	1,934
10.5	9.9	8.2	7.7	7.6	7.5	7.4	7.3
60.8	61.6	65.7	66.3	66.5	66.7	66.9	67.1
48.0	45.0	34.0	31.0	29.0	27.0	25.0	23.0
64.0	77.5	92.3	96.3	97.3	95.0	97.0	97.0
1,527	1,456	1,040	1,060	970	860	840	840
390	594	370	380	350	320	320	330
491	482	370	370	360	360	390	440
23,008	18,799	14,800	15,200	15,300	13,200	12,500	13,100
9,794	6,714	6,000	6,300	5,600	5,400	5,100	5,400
49.0	48.0	46.0	45.0	44.7	43.9	42.2	40.3
618	655	774	812	867	910	961	1002
6,296	7,364	9,464	10,318	11,215	12,302	13,350	14,373
203,334	232,417	311,520	342,682	378,131	412,477	448,813	481,071
8,733	10,612	13,818	14,787	16,573	17,903	19,992	21,415
2,316	2,681	3,536	3,408	3,725	3,766	4,051	5,660
32.30	31,56	32.92	33.21	33.72	33.53	33.62	33.47
23.28	21.90	22.54	23.17	22.82	23.04	22.45	22.46
56,825	64,268	78,348	80,954	84,269	91,709	97,373	102,516
67.97	63.60	61.31	62.60	63.42	64.46	64.94	65.97
3502	3768	4349	4680	4995	5232	5621	5831
23,391	41,320	83,032	93,841	107,409	120,230	130,979	153,300
2016	2498	3773	3927	4504	4625	5113	5833
1878	2353	3541	3688	4253	5365	4841	5518
5682.4	7881.9	11728.3	12186.2	13214.3	13354.1	14677.2	15571.3
4368.2	5670.9	11708.7	12171.1	13183.7	13287.4	14275.8	15473.5

Appendix Table VII.2

Gross Fixed Capital Formation by Plan Period (1976-92)
(Million RO)

Activities	1976-80				1981-85			
	Private	Public	Total	%	Private	Public	Total	%
Goods Producing Sectors								
1. (a) PDO Development								
Expenditure	132.0	204.7	336.7	20.0	304.9	455.7	760.6	19.5
(b) Other Oil Sectors	65.3	0.0	65.3	3.9	272.1	1.9	274.0	7.0
2. Natural Gas	0.0	20.7	20.7	1.2	0.0	38.7	38.7	1.0
3. Mining & Quarrying	1.3	11.7	13.0	0.8	0.0	64.3	64.3	1.7
4. Education	0.0	26.9	26.9	1.6	0.0	163.8	163.8	4.2
5. Health	0.0	22.1	22.1	1.3	0.0	71.7	71.7	1.8
6. Housing	187.0	28.2	215.2	12.8	282.9	98.6	381.5	9.8
7. Roads	0.0	192.7	192.7	11.5	0.0	281.8	281.8	7.2
8. Electricity	0.0	102.6	102.6	6.1	0.0	140.7	140.7	3.6
9. Water	0.0	27.7	27.7	1.6	0.0	93.1	93.1	2.4
10. Manufacturing	69.1	6.9	76.0	4.5	99.9	76.5	176.4	4.5
11. Agriculture & Fisheries	12.9	18.6	31.5	1.9	30.0	43.0	73.0	1.9
12. Other	27.3	523.5	550.8	32.8	147.7	1,226.1	1,373.8	35.3
13. Total	494.9	1,186.3	1,681.2	100.0	1,137.5	2,755.9	3,893.4	100.0
Percentage to the GDP	8.1	19.3	27.4		7.9	19.2	27.1	

Source: Oman, *Statistical Year Books.*

1986-90				1991-92			
Private	Public	Total	%	Private	Public	Total	%
339.3	524.5	863.8	29.2	189.9	284.9	474.8	33.4
165.5	0.4	165.9	5.6	57.8	0.0	57.8	4.1
0.0	74.8	74.8	2.5	0.0	51.6	51.6	3.6
0.0	7.8	7.8	0.3	0.0	3.8	3.8	0.3
0.0	107.6	107.6	3.6	0.0	27.2	27.2	1.9
0.0	100.0	100.0	3.4	0.0	24.9	24.9	1.8
199.2	67.3	266.5	9.0	138.6	21.3	159.9	11.3
0.0	144.9	144.9	4.9	0.0	33.6	33.6	2.4
0.0	110.5	110.5	3.7	0.0	42.7	42.7	3.0
0.0	36.1	36.1	1.2	0.0	60.4	60.4	4.3
93.1	25.6	118.7	4.0	49.9	6.5	56.4	4.0
27.9	40.9	68.8	2.3	17.3	21.3	38.6	2.7
126.0	764.8	890.8	30.1	55.5	333.8	389.8	27.4
951.0	2,005.2	2,956.2	100.0	509.0	912.0	1,421.0	100.0
5.9	12.5	18.4		6.1	10.9	17.0	

Appendix VIII

Closing speech by Mohamed bin Musa Al-Yousef, Minister of State for Development Affairs, to the Conference: Vision for Oman's Economy: OMAN 2020, 4 June 1995

I have pleasure to meet you once again, at the end of the activities of the Vision Conference for Oman's Economy: OMAN 2020. You have followed with us the deliberations and discussions of this conference, which have been characterised from its first session by good comradeship, open and frank discussions and innovative suggestions.

I have the honour to review with you the most important recommendations that have been agreed during the Conference's sessions.

First: Oman has laid, in just 25 years, sufficient foundations for becoming a dynamic, diversified and self sustaining economy. The Omani people thus have good reason for taking pride in their country's achievements.

Second: It is important to emphasise that the vision for Omani economy aims above all to preserve Oman's values, and to maintain, as a minimum, the current level of per capita income in real terms and to strive to double it by 2020.

Third: The major foundations of the future policies may be summarised as follows:

1 Developing our human resources and the capabilities of the Omani people to cope with the national economy's requirements. That, in turn, requires an environment that promotes, nurtures and disseminates knowledge and ideas and encourages the exchange of views. This will provide the flexibility needed to accommodate and manage technological change to meet the requirements of the labout market, where the labour force can earn a living commensurate with performance and productivity.

The comprehensive strategy of human resources development will focus on provision of primary health care and primary education for all Omanis, delivered by cost-effective and efficient systems.

2 Providing a stable macro-economic environment to develop a private sector capable of using Oman's human and natural resources in ways that are efficient and environmentally safe. That requires restoring fiscal balance, over the Fifth Five-Year Plan (1996-2000), through reduction of public expenditure, accumulation of a budget surplus and the streamlining of various forms of subsidies, broadening the base of Government revenues and increasing the efficiency and productivity of public activities.

3 Sharing the responsibility of economic development with a competitive and developed private sector, providing a prominent role for the private sector as the primary engine of economic growth, and maintaining a continuous dialogue with the Government. This can be achieved through the following:

- Promoting mechanisms and institutions that will foster a shared vision and policies between both sectors.

- Implementing privatisation plans as necessary at a pace consistent with the financial and managerial capabilities of the private sector.

- Eliminating administrative barriers facing the free entry of private capital in various activities.

- Upgrading laws to ensure free competition, equal opportunity and promote public awareness of this strategy of private sector development.

4 Facilitating the appropriate climate for economic diversification. The dependence on a single income source such as oil, as is currently the case in Oman, makes it imperative to focus on developing various export-led industries. Identifying and exploiting our comparative advantages are important elements of our diversification strategy. The unique geographical location and natural resources of the Sultanate provide great potential for the development of agriculture, fisheries, tourism, minerals, telecommunications and tradeable services. It is also necessary to move quickly to benefit from the emerging peace in the Middle East and the proliferation of regional and international trading agreements. All these policies confirm the importance that we attach to enhancing the development of a diversified and internationally competitive economy, and to achieve, at the same time, our national objectives.

5 Having always viewed improving the living standard of the Omani citizen and levels of development among regions as basic development objectives, the Government of His Majesty Sultan Qaboos bin Said, Sultan of Oman, will continue to act to achieve this equity in ways that encourage individual and collective initiative and responsibility. All the development policies will be designed to reduce disparities in living standards between regions and income groups to ensure that all the citizens share the benefits of the development process, and to provide the social security needed to protect deserving groups.

6 There is no doubt that many elements of the envisioned strategy will improve productivity more than enough to offset some of the sacrifices that may be required over the medium term as a result of implementing that strategy. In addition, this strategy will also allow the Omani people to improve their living standards in a stable and prosperous climate.

This Conference represents the first step in our discussions through the different Omani channels, so as to realise the vision for Oman's economy. The recommendations of this Conference will be transformed from a mere document of intentions to an approved policy that will provide guidance to the Government in preparing the Fifth Five-Year Plan, and the plans that will follow in the 21st century.

It is important to state that the vision objectives and policies, despite appropriate preparation, will need to be reviewed from time to time in the context of developments and global economic conditions.

Finally, I would like to thank all of you – your Highnesses, your Excellencies and honourable guests – for participating with us in this major economic event, which we hope will illuminate our road to the 21st century, so that the Sultanate will advance with yet more confidence and pride under the wise leadership of His Majesty Sultan Qaboos bin Said, Sultan of Oman.

Assalamo alaikom wa rahmato Allahi wa barakatoh
(Peace be upon you, may God bless all of you)

Selected Bibliography

Alvin Y. So, *Social Change and Development: Directions in Development Theory* (SAGE Publications, Newbury Park, London and Delhi, 1990).

Balassa, B., *Change and Challenge in the World Economy* (Macmillan, London, 1985).

Bauer, P.T., *Dissent on Development* (Weidenfeld and Nicholson, London, 1976).

British Petroleum Co., *BP Statistical Review of World Energy* (London, June 1994).

Clements, F.A., *Oman, The Reborn Land* (Longman, London and New York, 1980).

Corbridge Stuart, *Capitalist World Development* (Macmillan, London, 1988).

Dicken, Peter, *Global Shift: Internationalization of Economic Activity* (Paul Chapman Publishing Ltd, London, 1992).

Economist Intelligence Unit, *Country Profile: Oman, Yemen, 1993/94* (EIU, London, 1993).

Findlay, Allan M., *The Arab World* (Routledge, New York, 1994).

Gwynne, Robert N., *New Horizons? Third World Industrialization in an International Framework* (Longman Scientific & Technical, London, 1990).

Hansen, Bent, *Political Economy of Poverty, Equity and Growth, Egypt and Turkey* (Oxford University Press for the World Bank, 1991).

Henry, Barkey (ed.), *The Politics of Economic Reform in the Middle East* (St. Martin's Press, New York, 1992).

Hunt, Diana, *Economic Theories of Development. An Analysis of Competing Paradigms* (Harvester Wheatsheaf, New York, London and Toronto, 1989).

Jenkins, R.O., *Transnational Corporations and Uneven Development* (International Thompson, London, 1987).

Meier, Gerald M., *Leading Issues in Economic Development* (Oxford University Press, New York, 1989).

Middle East Economic Survey, Vol.37, No.35 (Cypress, 1994).

Nazir, Pervaiz, *Local Development in the Global Economy* (Avebury Gower Publications, Hampshire, 1991).

Oman, Charles P. and Wignaraja, Ganeshan, *The Post-War Evolution of Development* (Macmillan, London, 1991)

Oman, Sultanate of, *Statistical Year Book* (Oman, 1972-).

Oman, Sultanate of, *The Annual Statistical Report 1994* (Ministry of Health, Oman, 1994).

Oman, Sultanate of, *The First Five Year Development Plan, 1976-1980* (Oman, 1976).

Oman, Sultanate of, *The Second Five-Year Development Plan, 1981-1985* (Oman, 1981).

Oman, Sultanate of, *The Third Five-Year Development Plan, 1986-1990* (Oman, 1986).

Oman, Sultanate of, *The Fourth Five-Year Development Plan, 1991-1995* (Oman, 1991).

Oman, Sultanate of, *Preliminary Results of the General Census of Population, Housing and Establishments, December 1993* (Oman, 1993).

Oman, Sultanate of, *Oman 2020: Vision for Oman's Economy* (Oman, 1995)

OPEC, *OPEC at a Glance* (1993).

Political Risk Services, *International Country Risk Guide*, Vol.15, No.1 (PRS, Syracuse, 1994).

Pomfret, Richard, *Diverse Paths of Economic Development* (Harvester Wheatsheaf, New York and London, 1992).

Pridham, B.R. (ed.), *Oman: Economic, Social and Strategic Developments* (Croom Helm, London and Sydney, 1987).

Rostow, W.W., *The Stages of Economic Growth: A Non-Communist Manifesto* (Cambridge University Press, London, 1960).

Schuurman, F.J. (ed.), *Beyond the Impasse: New Directions in Development Theory* (Zed Books, London, 1993).

Seers, Dudley, 'Massive Transfers and Mutual Interests', *World Development*, Vol.9, No.6.

Thirlwall, A.P., *Growth and Development with Special Reference to Developing Economies* (Macmillan, London, 1990).

Todaro, Michael P., *Economic Development in the Third World* (Longman, New York and London, 1992).

UNDP, *Human Development Report 1994* (Oxford University Press, New York, 1994).

UNESCO, *Statistical Yearbook* (UNESCO, Paris, 1984, 1989, 1991).

UNICEF, *The Progress of Nations* (UNICEF, New York, 1994).

Warren, B., *Imperialism: Pioneer of Capitalism* (London, 1980).

Waterston, Albert, *Development Planning: Lessons of Experience* (Johns Hopkins University Press, Baltimore and London, 1982).

Wilber, Charles K. et al, *The Political Economy of Development and Under-Development* (McGraw-Hill Inc., New York, 1982).

World Bank, *The East Asian Miracle: Economic Growth & Public Policy* (Oxford University Press, New York, 1993).

World Bank, *Oman: Review of Recurrent Public Expenditure in Public Health and Education, August 1994* (1994).

World Bank, *Social Indicators of Development* (Johns Hopkins University Press, Baltimore and London, 1992, 1994).

World Bank, *Sultanate of Oman: Sustainable Growth and Economic Diversification, December 23, 1993* (1993).

World Bank, *World Development Indicators 1992: Data on Diskette* (World Bank, Washington D.C., 1992).

World Bank, *World Development Report 1994: Infrastructure for Development* (Oxford University Press, New York, 1994).

World Bank, *World Tables 1994* (Johns Hopkins University Press, Baltimore and London, 1994).

INDEX